Alone in the Crowd?

Social Isolation of Seniors in Care Facilities

ᘓ

Association
of Advocates
for Care Reform

Vancouver, BC
Seattle, Washington

Canadian Cataloguing in Publication Data
Alone in a crowd?
ISBN 0-89716-718-X
1. Aged--Social conditions. 2. Social isolation.
3. Aged--Institutional care.
I. Association of Advocates for Care Reform.
HQ1061.A66 1997   305.26   C97-910912-4

Project directed by Charmaine Spencer and Mary Hill
Editor: Suzanne Bastedo
Book Design and Production: Fiona Raven
Cover Design: Kelly Brooks

First printing November 1997

PEANUT BUTTER PUBLISHING

Suite 212 - 1656 Duranleau Street • Granville Island
• Vancouver, BC V6H 3S4 • 604-688-0320 •
226 2nd Avenue West • Seattle, WA 98119 • 206-281-5965
e mail: pnutpub@aol.com
Internet: http://www.pbpublishing.com

Printed in Canada

Funding provided by Health Canada — New Horizons
Partners in Aging Program

Acknowledgements

Many thanks to the people who contributed to this handbook:

- the residents who shared their experiences for the research project

- the family and friends, volunteers, staff, and management of the care facilities involved in the research project

- the volunteer research assistants who conducted the interviews

- Barbara Oleschuk of New Horizons/Health Canada

- the research project Advisory Committee, eight of whom are seniors

- the Steering Committee which took major responsibility for the work

- Darja Kiara, the project coordinator

- the Board of Directors, Association of Advocates for Care Reform, 1995 to 1997

Table of Contents

Preface

In the summer of 1995, the Association of Advocates for Care Reform (ACR) discussed developing a resource manual. Through our work with seniors, we realized that there was not much information about life in care facilities. ACR members found that many seniors were worried about having to move into a care facility and some seniors already in one seemed lonely and despondent.

We wanted to understand more about what it was like to live in a care facility, and were particularly concerned about residents who believed they were forgotten. We decided to go to the source and to call on the knowledge and experience of seniors who lived in care facilities, their family and friends, and care facility staff, volunteers, and management.

In February 1996, ACR applied to Health Canada's New Horizons Partners in Aging

Program for funding, obtained a grant, and hired a project coordinator. The project's goals were: (1) to hear from seniors about their experiences living in care facilities; (2) to look at the causes of social isolation; (3) to gather suggestions about how to reduce social isolation of seniors in care facilities; and (4) to create a handbook about social isolation and distribute it widely to those interested in or affected by social isolation.

This handbook contains a number of suggestions which we hope government officials, social services, medical professionals, management and staff of care facilities will think about when designing buildings, programs, and services for seniors.

Alone In A Crowd? will be distributed to health departments, libraries, information centres, and all BC long-term care facilities.

Special thanks to Health Canada and the seniors who made this handbook a reality.

Amy Freeman, BSW
ACR President,
December 1995 to April 1997

ADVISORY COMMITTEE

Douglas Armitage   Lisa Schwabe
Amy Freeman   Helen Shore
Esme Gooderham   Charmaine Spencer
Mary Hill   Kay Stovold
Angela Johnston   Lesley Taylor
Bill Nicholls   Daisy Webster
Barbara Oleschuk   Joyce Wright

STEERING COMMITTEE

Phase One: Phase Two:
Amy Freeman   Amy Freeman
Mary Hill   Mary Hill
Lesley Taylor   Charmaine Spencer

PROJECT COORDINATOR

Darja Kiara

PROJECT EVALUATOR

Diana Tindall

All about this handbook

What This Handbook Is About

This handbook describes life from the perspectives of seniors living in care facilities and of those involved with them. It describes how meaningful relationships for people who live in care facilities can flourish or falter, and how some people become socially isolated even with many other people around them.

This handbook is based on a research project which ACR carried out in 1996-97 with funding from Health Canada/New Horizons. The project included detailed interviews with 49 seniors (11 men and 38 women) living in four care facilities for seniors in the Greater Vancouver area, as well as personal and telephone interviews with 51 family and friends of seniors living in care facilities, and care facility staff, management, and volunteers.

Several words are generally used to describe people in the later stages of life — for example, "elders," "old," "senior," and "the elderly." There is no one ideal word, just as there is no agreement about age. To a care facility, a senior may be someone who is at least 55; to the federal government, a senior may be someone who is 65. To someone who is 87, none of these so-called seniors may seem old at all.

In this handbook, the word seniors refers to the people whose voices we hear throughout the handbook. They range in age from 71 to 98 years old.

Why Care About Social Isolation In Care Facilities?

If you are reading this, perhaps you are concerned about a family member or friend who is living in a care facility and who seems isolated. She or he may seem to have few opportunities to connect with others, share, touch, or be intimate. He or she may seem to lack freedom and independence.

Perhaps you just want to learn more about relationships in care facilities, whether among residents, between residents and staff or volunteers, or between residents and family members. You may be identifying with your own possible future; you may want to make life in a care facility better for yourself and others, too. Or you might simply believe that being connected with other people gives health benefits to everyone.

With the Best of Intentions

The research project shows that the residents, family, friends, staff, and volunteers often have very different views about social isolation. The seniors who live in the four care facilities talk about needing privacy, finding socializing outside of activity programs difficult, needing to be heard, and wanting freedom of choice.

In contrast, families, staff, and volunteers talk about wanting to see residents kept busier with programs. With the best of intentions, families, staff, and volunteers may be trying to do what the residents do not want or need.

Before we can respond effectively to social isolation, we need to learn about what helps make relationships in care facilities possible and what makes them more difficult. For a long time, the working title of this handbook was *Someone To Talk To*, but this research project shows that doing something about social isolation in care facilities is more than simply finding someone to talk to. "Alone in a crowd" is a phrase we heard often from the seniors who talked with us, and it became the title of this handbook about social isolation.

Who This Handbook Is For

This handbook is for several different groups of people: seniors who live in care facilities now and those who may be going into a care facility sometime in the near future; their family and friends; staff and management of care facilities; potential and current volunteers in care facilities; and people in the community who are involved with seniors.

While the focus here is on seniors, social isolation does not happen only to seniors in care facilities. It also happens to the younger adults who may live there. The information and ideas contained in this handbook may be useful for anyone living, working, or volunteering in a care facility.

How to Use This Handbook

This handbook is divided into sections so that you can quickly look up information which interests you. The handbook starts with a brief look at what we mean by social isolation and at some of the issues involved. Then the three main parts focus on what the residents and others say about: (1) life in a care facility; (2) meaningful relationships; (3) extra challenges. These parts feature answers the residents give to questions asked in the research project. Also included are brief descriptions of what family, friends, staff, and volunteers interviewed say in answer to the questions they were asked in the research project.

So that you can find ideas for action quickly, each part ends with a summary and suggestions. The suggestions from the residents, family, friends, staff, and volunteers are organized in checklists which contain background information on various issues as well as ideas for what you can do to make a difference to seniors who live in care facilities.

The next two parts of the handbook are a short section on the dignity of risk and an epilogue, both of which may be of special interest to anyone interested in some of the challenges facing care facilities today, and in policy and planning.

At the end of the handbook are two appendices. In Appendix 1, you will find information about the research project and the residents who participated. In Appendix 2, you will find information about helpful books, articles, groups, and projects.

What You Can Expect to Find

Throughout this handbook, there are many suggestions for ways to make a difference to seniors who live in care facilities. Some suggestions are fairly easy to carry out; others may need to be put into policy and planning for facilities in the future.

You will not find blame in this handbook. When seniors look or feel socially isolated, it is natural for people to want to hold someone responsible. Families, friends, and staff may want to make things better, but may have difficulty understanding all the reasons behind the situation. Some try to make the person responsible for feeling alone or sad. He may hear comments like: "If only you'd try harder . . ." or she may hear: "If you wouldn't be so stubborn . . ."

But the finger gets pointed at others as well. Staff are told: "If only there were more activities, the residents wouldn't feel so alone." Management is told: "If only you did more with the money there is." Government and other funders are told: "If only there was more funding." While there is some truth in each of these statements, they don't necessarily bring about change for seniors who are socially isolated in care facilities.

This handbook does not provide all the answers to reduce or prevent social isolation of seniors, but sheds light on the fact that some people have difficulties in care facilities and that there are things that can be done to make a difference to them.

What is social isolation?

VIGNETTE: Her family knows her as Fiona. To the staff she is Miss G. She is 79 and has lived in a care facility for three years. Two years ago her only brother died. The staff cannot remember any visitors appearing for over a year. The staff say that the last visitor was a minister who came "reluctantly" and that during the visit Miss G. was "rude and bad-tempered" and complained that the minister didn't come often enough. Miss G. talks about waiting to die. The staff find it exhausting to listen to her constant grumbling and say that they must force themselves to stay with her longer than absolutely necessary.

* * *

Social isolation can be looked at from two sometimes very different perspectives: (1) the resident's point of view — does she or he feel isolated? (2) according to others involved with the person — does he or she seem isolated? These points of view may agree — for instance, in the case of Miss G., when she and others feel that she is socially isolated. These points of view may also differ — for instance, when others think that the person is isolated and wants change, but the person does not.

Then comes the most important question and the focus of this handbook: What does the person want? Sometimes people decide that someone who spends more than a certain number of hours in her or his room is socially isolated. Sometimes people decide that someone is not socializing enough. From that point on, the person is treated as though he or she has a problem that needs to be fixed.

The "diagnosis" often focuses on someone who:
- cries a lot
- acts out, yells, or screams
- complains often, or never complains
- looks depressed, sad, or withdrawn
- has few or no visitors
- stays in his or her room

This assessment is sometimes made without checking to see how the person feels. The well-meaning "treatment" may be to add more medicines, more people, more activities, or more events to the person's life.

However, looking from the "outside" and focusing only on what *seems* to be ignores the personal aspect of relationships. It also ignores the fact that this person did not land on the earth yesterday. He or she has already had a long life, often through 80 or more years.

Only the person can say what her or his "inside" life is like, not only physical condition, but also life experiences, lifestyle, personality, skills, and strengths. Is she satisfied with life? Is he content with how much contact he has with others? You might hear that he feels lonely or forgotten. Or you may be surprised to hear that she is not a "joiner," is in fact quite happy to be in her room, and socializes on her own terms.

As this handbook shows, people who live in care facilities can have many kinds of relationships. Their relationships may be with people they are in contact with every day or only occasionally. Some relationships will be meaningful to them and some will not.

To ask about relationships which are meaningful, the questionnaires in the research project use the terms "deep friendship," "special relationship," or "trusted friend." In this handbook, a meaningful relationship is one which contains a sense of trust, friendliness, caring about and respecting the other person's wishes, wanting to understand the other person, and wishing the person well. It also means respecting personal boundaries.

The staff may see one side of the resident, families another, and friends yet another. For that reason, before saying that a person is socially isolated and doing anything to change that, it is important first to talk with the person, and then to talk with as many family, friends, staff, and volunteers involved in the person's life as possible, while always respecting the person's right to confidentiality and privacy.

WHAT YOU CAN DO TO MAKE A DIFFERENCE TO . . . someone you think may be socially isolated

- First and foremost, be aware that the person is the best judge about whether she or he is socially isolated

- Respect the person for all her or his choices, including the choice to be, or not to be, more sociable

- Before deciding that someone is socially isolated and doing anything to change that, first talk with the person, and then, with the person's permission, talk with as many other people involved in the person's life as possible

Part 1

What the residents and others say about life in a care facility

VIGNETTE: Mrs. R. told her family that the staff was constantly reminding her to wear her hearing aid. The trouble was that even when wearing it, she could not distinguish what was being said among all the noises in the lounge. Several times she answered questions in a way which got puzzled looks. Then she realized that she had misunderstood the remarks. They all thought she was confused — that is, demented. After a while she gave up trying to look interested and stayed in her room. It took too much energy to try to cope. She has asked to sit alone in the dining room.

* * *

Introduction

This first section of the handbook features what the seniors involved in the research project say about living in care facilities, from when they first moved in to how it felt after living there for some time. They talk about what's important; what's positive; what's negative; what they miss most; what decisions they can make; how much control they feel they have; whether they often feel happy, sad, or satisfied; whether they often feel angry or lonely, and whether they do anything to feel better. Also included are brief looks at what family, friends, staff, and volunteers say.

Most of the residents lived in a private household before moving into the care facility. More than half lived alone, while about one third shared a home with others, usually a spouse, but occasionally with a child or a friend. One quarter of the residents had already lived in another care facility or a hospital before they moved into their current home. While on average, the residents had lived in the care facility for about three years, some had moved into the care facility only a few months before the interview, and others had lived in the care facility for as long as 14 years.

A. Withdrawing from Others

Like Mrs. R., one third of the residents say that they sometimes have difficulty mixing with others, and some cope with the many changes in their lives by withdrawing from others for short or long periods of time.

Some describe physical difficulties — such as with speech or walking — but for many, the difficulties have to do with personality and way of approaching life:

> "The 'claustrophobic' conditions of living with so many others."

> "I'm in rebellion against my son who put me here."

> "I get frustrated with other old people. I tend to avoid some of them."

Each senior living in a care facility has a unique personality and has had a unique lifestyle and life experience, all affecting how she or he copes with changes. In care facilities, where there are many people, there are also many kinds of personalities, lifestyles, and life experiences. Some people may be able to focus on what is still possible; for others, it's more of a struggle.

People who seek out relationships

Some seniors seek out relationships and don't withdraw for long from other people. For them, continuing existing relationships and starting new relationships in a care facility, where there are lots of people, may be easy:

"It's not hard to get to meet people because you can talk to anyone here."

"I get up every day and communicate with people."

Others find it harder to meet and get to know others. They may want to start new relationships in the care facility, but are unable, for a variety of reasons:

"I don't even know my next-door neighbour!"

A senior may have several meaningful relation-ships with family or friends in the community which continue after she or he moves into the care facility. Starting new relationships in the care facility may just be a matter of time, the longer he or she lives there. For a person with this type of personality or approach to life, even becoming disabled may mean finding out what relationships are possible in the new way of life. This kind of person usually does not withdraw from others for long, but finds it possible to have and keep relationships. For the person who is usually out-going to withdraw for a long time would signal to others that there might be a problem.

People who prefer being solitary

Other people prefer being solitary. For them, living in a care facility among many other people may be difficult, especially at first. About one in five residents say that they want to be left alone.

Some lived alone for a long time before coming to the care facility and find adjusting to other people and routines difficult:

"I came here late in life — I'm used to living alone."

Some may have led very private lives before moving into the care facility, perhaps seeing a few family members or long-time friends:

"I tended to keep to myself."

Some may have always found it hard to make friends or to get along with others:

"I didn't suffer fools gladly."

"I won't answer any questions. Let's just leave it at that!"

Or the person may need time:

"I find it hard to express myself and often go a long time before I come around."

People who prefer to be solitary do not change the personalities of a lifetime and start wanting many people in their lives. Many say that they want to be left alone:

| "I'm a real loner. I do my own thing." |

Some residents are solitary not so much by choice as because they are fearful of other residents — for instance, those who wander from room to room at night, or who go through other people's belongings, or who have dementia:

"I avoid 'disturbed' residents."

"I stay by myself — I want nothing to do with those people."

What staff and volunteers say about people who prefer being solitary

Staff and volunteers interviewed say that seniors who prefer being solitary can adjust well to life in a care facility, especially after they have been there for a while and have had a chance to find out how to make and use the time they need alone.

According to staff and volunteers, residents who spend much of their time alone are still active in many different ways. Some do not usually choose to be in the more public parts of the care facility, but may listen to music or radio talk shows, watch TV, read, do crossword puzzles, watch others, or knit, to name just some activities.

Withdrawing is a way of coping with change

Moving into a care facility is a big change, whatever a person's personality. Some seniors can plan when and how they enter a care facility. The move becomes another chosen and planned life experience — like marriage, for example. But like any other major change, everyone, whether outgoing or not, needs time and support to adjust to the new surroundings and lifestyle. Withdrawing from others, whether for a short or a long time, is one way of coping with the change.

People differ in how much they trust others, but those who have recently moved into a care facility are much more likely to resist, refuse, or simply be cautious about developing relationships for the first weeks or months.

Unfortunately, that is exactly the time when staff and other residents are forming their first impressions of the person. Unless staff are aware that relationships and trust take time to build, they may label a new resident "withdrawn" or "depressed" or even "paranoid" and other residents may decide that the person is unsociable. This adds to the loneliness and stress new residents may already be experiencing.

A senior whose move is unplanned may be more likely to become socially isolated and may need extra time, consideration, and support to cope with the changes. Moving to a care facility may happen suddenly — after a fall, for instance — and the person may not have had a chance to say good-bye to her or his home. The person may feel he or she has little or no control over living in the care facility.

Changes in health can affect how sociable residents feel. As Part 3 will show, residents often experience a major change in health while living in the facility. Some find these physical changes — such as blindness, partial or total deafness, being incontinent, or having to use a walker or cane, or seemingly minor conditions like coughing — embarrassing, and withdraw from others. Whatever the personality or previous life experience, someone who experiences changes like this may withdraw from others in an attempt to cope.

The person who is bedridden in a care facility may also spend much time alone and talk mainly with staff. This person may or may not be choosing to be alone, but cannot easily get out to meet people or join in activities:

"I'm unable to get up alone . . . to chitchat with others."

Some residents who spend much time alone say that they are not interested in other people's lives or don't want to become entangled:

> "When I meet others in a social group, I keep away from gossiping."

> "I don't want to get too involved."

Another life experience which particularly affects seniors who live in care facilities is the death of friends and family. Some have already lost people they care about, and hesitate to start new relationships, for fear of losing them too:

> "I don't make friends anymore . . . they keep dying on me."

B. A Mixed Blessing

For many seniors, moving into a care facility is the only way to have their physical needs met. But living in a care facility can mean changing almost everything in their lives. It is no surprise that many seniors find living in a care facility a mixed blessing.

Moving to a care facility means communal living. The person is expected to share meals and activities. She or he is living in one room — and may have to share that, too. All other living space is communal.

Most people are not used to this way of living. There are usually only a few times in North American society where people live in close quarters with others unrelated to them — going to summer camp as children, or living in a dormitory at college or university, or joining a religious or ethnic community. People generally choose to be in these situations, however, and can leave whenever they want. For the senior who now lives in a care facility, leaving may not be possible.

Living in a care facility can mean giving up long-time activities and connections with the outside world. Friends and family can visit but they cannot follow. A senior's relationships with all the people familiar to everyday life — such as the doctor, the homecare providers, the hairdresser or barber, the letter carrier, the clerk at the grocery store, or staff at the bank — may now end suddenly.

C. What's Important

The residents say that there are many things important in their lives. For three in five, family and friends are most important:

"Get up and around and have a smile when the kids come to visit."

"Visiting with my [family] as much as possible and going out with them."

"Church because I get to see my friends on a more regular basis."

"Just being here with my wife."

They also focus on being able to do things and be independent:

"The freedom here to do what is important and yet I'm cared for — perhaps a much better way than the Ritz!"

"Glad that I can still do things independently."

"Having time in my own room."

"I like to get out."

"I love shopping — buying clothes."

Whatever helps the residents "go home" again, even just for a short while, can also be very important:

"I like to go back home and cook."

"To get back with my family."

For some, spirituality or faith is very important:

"Faith and food — a very strong belief in God."

"Learning to obey and trust in the Lord."

"Living a Christian life."

For others, simply "hanging in there" is important:

"Getting through the day ... don't look forward to day after day, but I take it as it comes."

"Just to be alive and to do the best I can every day."

"Not to get much older!"

"Waiting for the Lord."

Health is also mentioned frequently:

"Not to have pain."

"Still having my sight."

"If I was stronger, I would work in the garden, and I don't mind housework."

Even the basic necessities are important:

"My food and safety here at the home."

"Three meals — a bed — medicine."

A few find little in their lives that's important:

"I don't know — it's the same day after day."

"I don't want to go on living. I can't do anything."

What staff and volunteers say is important to residents

Many of the residents focus on family, independence, and day-to-day survival as the important things in life. Staff and volunteers interviewed emphasize family and independence less, and how basic human needs are met in the care facility more. For example, they talk about the importance of eating, health care, family, having someone to talk with. They suggest ways the care facility could be more homelike — having a comfortable, relaxed atmosphere, with choices and respect for all residents. Some staff and volunteers also add that they feel entertainment and outings are important to residents.

D. What's Positive

About one quarter of the residents say that after living in the care facility for a few months, they saw positive changes in their lives:

"We feel lucky we can be together." (a married couple)

"I love my private room and bathroom."

"I like to be with people."

"Didn't want to stay by myself any more."

"Can be among people my own age."

"Here, everything is included."

"They [staff] help with my problems."

When asked about the highlights of a typical day, many of the residents say that they look forward to the regular routine. The routine may be what's going on in the care facility — a regular exercise program, a cooking class — or the resident's own routine — watching favourite TV programs, reading the Bible. Some residents join whatever is going on.

Some of the residents say that their highlight is having plenty to do, whether they prefer to be alone, or spend a lot of time in their own rooms, or often join in organized activities:

"I'm keeping very busy."

"I'm a great reader — never lonely with a book."

"I'm trying to write a book."

Some look forward to being around people:

"Company — I just enjoy the daily routine of the home."

"Chatting with people in the building."

"Enjoy the care that staff show, particularly in the morning, checking that I am OK."

Others say that they enjoy having their own room:

"Being able to shut the door."

Several people who are bedridden say their highlight may simply be changing position:

"Sit up three to four hours of the day."

Some say that meals are the highlight of their average day, but very few mention visitors, which may not happen every day.

What family, friends, staff, and volunteers say about what's positive

About one third of the family and friends interviewed feel that the move has been generally positive for the senior with whom they are involved: he or she is safe, physically cared for, and has many people to talk with and many activities to do. Some mention the significant compromises the senior must make in the care facility — such as being able to keep some personal possessions, but having to fit them into a small space, or being able to have visitors, but having no place to talk with them privately.

Staff and volunteers also say that they feel there are many positives for seniors living in care facilities. Several add that sometimes the person needs time to adjust before the changes can be called positive. Like family and friends, many staff and volunteers believe that the person is better off in the care facility, especially for physical care and safety. A few also mention that they think some women "blossom" while living in a care facility as they are no longer responsible for family, spouse, or home.

E. What's Negative

At the same time, one quarter of the residents say that the changes in their lives are negative since they moved into the care facility.

Many have experienced a decline in physical and mental health. This may have first started when the person was living in the community and continues in the care facility:

"It's harder to get out."

"My legs are heavy when I walk — I get out of breath."

"It's difficult to talk."

"My condition is worsening."

"Eyesight worse — not able to get around as much."

Some, especially those who are blind or have visual impairments, say that the most negative part of their lives is that they have become increasingly dependent:

"I need help to do anything now."

Many say that they find it hard trying to adjust to the routine and people of the facility:

"You have to remember the names of all the staff."

"Having to live in one room and among so many people is hardest to get used to."

"Being tied down to a schedule."

"Lack of privacy — hard to have people check on you even though it's necessary."

Some have not found activities to replace what they used to do:

"I can't do anything — loved to clean and work and can't do any of that here."

"I can't cook my own meals."

"Doing nothing all day and not having my own things."

"I moved in too early."

Some say that they have no highlights in their days:

"It's rather monotonous — each day is much the same as the next!"

"I sit on my fanny — eat — not much else you can do."

"No highlights, always monotonous — same from morning 'til night."

"No highlights — it's dead."

In adjusting to life in the care facility, some have withdrawn or changed how they deal with others:

"The days pass, and I sleep a lot."

"Just sit and think."

"I'm getting used to it — I've become crotchety."

A few feel negative about moving into the care facility:

> "Feeling that one has been dumped in the facility by relatives with the help of the doctor."

What family, friends, staff, and volunteers say about what's negative

Even though family and friends note many positive changes, two thirds see negative changes in the life of the senior with whom they are involved. In many ways, family, friends, staff, and volunteers echo what the seniors who live in the care facilities say — that for many residents, declining health and the effort needed to adjust to the care facility's routine makes living in a care facility a negative experience.

F. What's Missing Most

The residents say that they miss a lot from their previous lives — familiar people, their former homes, being able to live independently and make choices.

About half say that they most miss their spouses, homes, family and friends, church, and former neighbours:

> "Just being in my home."

"Having my own place, doing my own cooking, having my own furniture and things."

"Being able to putter around the house or yard."

"I miss staff from the other place I lived in."

They also miss entertaining guests in the way they used to do:

"Making drinks and food for visitors; entertaining not possible here."

"I can't entertain the way I used to . . . can't make coffee or tea. It's not a regular home."

"There's hardly space for more than two people in my room."

Some miss the routine of their former lives:

"Everything is different."

One third miss certain physical activities:

"Playing golf."

"I miss going camping."

"Used to go for exercises three times a week."

Many miss the physical things they used to own, as well as the space to put them in:

"The pictures."

"The hand-made coffee table my son built."

"Storage space."

A few say that although there are things they miss, change was already happening in their lives:

"I knew a lot of people in my apartment block, but a lot are now gone. Also I gradually was going out less and less even before I came here."

"There are fewer people to socialize with because many of my friends are ill or dead."

About one in five residents mention missing independence and privacy:

"Coming and going as I wish."

"A normal life."

"My freedom."

What family, friends, staff, and volunteers say is missing most

One quarter of the family and friends interviewed say that the seniors with whom they are involved talk about missing independence and freedom, as well as familiar people, places, and activities.

About a third of the family and friends note that the seniors miss being healthy and unencumbered by impairments in seeing, hearing, walking, or talking. Many family and friends focus on the decline in the person's physical abilities, remarking that he or she now needs extra help for grooming or getting out of bed.

About half of the family and friends say that the person mostly stays in her or his room and does not have enough to do. Many add that they think the person spends too much time in her or his room, and should make more of an effort to be sociable. Some say that staff should encourage the residents to be more active or sociable.

Staff and volunteers also say that many residents talk often about how much they miss their former homes and the physical things they owned. Staff add that since most seniors and staff in care facilities are female, male residents have to adjust to having many women around and may miss the company of other males.

Several family, friends, staff, and volunteers add that some residents miss speaking in their own language, and being able to understand what the other residents and staff are saying. In some care facilities an increasing number of residents or staff do not speak English as a first language.

G. "I'm old, but I'm still my own boss!"

The above quote is an example of how many of the residents feel about making decisions and having control over their lives.

Making decisions

Two out of three residents say that they are still making the big and small decisions that affect their lives. Many make most of their decisions about daily activities:

"Shopping for clothes. Hiring the handyDART. What meetings to attend at church."

"I make small decisions — take part in activities at my own pace."

"I decide what I want to do through the day."

"For my health — what I put in my body — to keep clean."

Some make decisions about how they will react to what's going on around them:

| "Not to stay angry — not to worry at it." |

Many residents make financial decisions about how their money is used and how it will be disposed of after they die:

"I have a will and trust fund."

"I look after my own money and make all the decisions."

"I try to keep my financial situation under control."

"Where my assets go."

One in four of the residents feel that they now make few if any decisions:

"Not many decisions to make any more."

"My niece looks after everything."

"I'm very aware of not doing anything wrong — making a mistake."

What family, friends, staff, and volunteers say about decision-making

Many family and friends interviewed say that the seniors with whom they are involved are very clear about making their own decisions, particularly about daily life in the care facility, and have little difficulty telling family or staff what they want.

Some seniors are less able or willing to make decisions or to speak out for themselves. Family and friends note that declining mental or physical health can make it difficult for some seniors to make decisions or tell other people what they want.

In some cases, family and friends say that instead of just going ahead with decisions, they always "ask" the person first, whether or not they are sure he or she understands. They feel that this consultation is an important part of showing respect for the person. Others say that over the years they have gradually taken over the person's decision-making, and that he or she seems to be happy with the arrangement.

Most of the staff and volunteers interviewed feel that there are many opportunities for the residents to make decisions. Only a few feel that the residents could make more decisions about what affects them directly — for instance, spiritual beliefs, personal grooming, what to eat, and what programs and entertainment are offered.

It is striking that many staff and volunteers use words such as "allowed," "permitted," or "encouraged" when they are talking about decisions made by the residents. Some staff and volunteers also add that they often "intervene" or "interpret" for residents who find it difficult to express or carry out their own choices.

Control

Just over one third of the residents say that they want more control of their lives in some areas.

Some wish they could control physical change or decline:

"Being able to talk better [after stroke]."

"Sight, and being able to get around better."

"More control over myself."

Some say that they want more control over how independent they are:

"Being able to go around and to travel on my own."

"Would like to do more volunteer work."

"Go to a show once in a while."

"Would like to drive a car."

"I would like to be able to sew for myself."

Some want more control over what they do and when they do it, especially when they do not feel there is enough choice offered by the care facility:

"I would like to sleep in occasionally."

"The menu [has] too much sameness — just apple pie, no cake."

"Would like to be able to say to care aides: 'Keep your hands off our stuff!'"

"Not to have to live crammed together."

Some want control over whether they are in the care facility at all:

"To go home — I'd be very happy to go home."

"I would like to move out to my own place."

"To decide how long I stay."

Some say that they have enough control over their lives:

"Very content the way it is — I have all the control I want."

"I don't think — so I'm happy — I'm still able to wash myself, and things like that."

"I'm satisfied the way it is ... I have as much as I can handle."

"I decided when I came in here this was going to be home, and it adjusts to my needs — when I'm going out they even will give me a key to get in."

What family, friends, staff, and volunteers say about control

Almost half of the family and friends interviewed say that they are not aware of any area where the residents with whom they are involved would like to have more control. Others note that some of the residents talk about wishing they had more control over declining health, whether or not they can return home, and when to have meals.

Staff and volunteers say that many residents talk about wanting more control over many of the daily routines of the care facility. Staff also add that the fixed routine of the care facility is sometimes in conflict with what the residents want to do. For instance, some residents want control over when and what to eat. Some also want more control over their table-mates — to choose for themselves the people with whom they sit. Some want to be "allowed" to eat in their rooms. Some want to choose when to get up and when to go to bed. Sometimes, the residents do not want to get up and eat at all, and resent having to. Staff say that residents especially would like more control over what they wear, and few are happy if staff make those choices.

H. Feelings

How do the residents feel about themselves, their lives, and living in a care facility? Like anyone else, at one time or another they may feel happy, satisfied, sad, angry, or lonely.

Happiness

More than four out of five of the residents say that they often feel happy. They identify many things to feel happy about:

"I like living here — it's 100 percent no problem — I'm very happy just living!"

"If I can make somebody laugh, I'm really happy."

"Music, flowers, people."

"No stress — security is good."

"I'm content — well taken care of."

"Happy that I can attend church."

"Fellowship with visitors and faith in the Lord and the care of the care workers."

Others feel happy in response to certain events, such as visits or outings:

"Yes, when I hear from my daughter."

"When I see one of my children."

"Relatives and friends, visiting outside, still able to get around."

Daily activities make some happy:

"Listening to music, singing and dancing with my walker."

"Watching TV."

"Knitting."

"Happy saying good-night to the cat."

"Getting together with others — Bible study, crafts, exercises with others."

"Watching games and playing games."

"Bingo, visiting all the residents, and TV."

Others make an effort to feel happy:

"It's no good feeling any other way — it doesn't help."

"Happy enough to get our three meals a day."

"I make an effort — it would be foolish not to try."

"Making the best of the situation — it's best in the long run that I'm here."

Some say that their happiness depends on what is going on in their lives:

"It depends on what turns up — sometimes I argue with my sister."

"I don't get depressed? [Of course I do.] What do you expect? I'm waiting to die!"

What family, friends, staff, and volunteers say about the residents being happy

About half of the family and friends interviewed feel the residents with whom they are involved are mostly happy. Staff and volunteers agree. Many feel that among the things that make the residents most happy are having physical care, activities to do, people to socialize with, and family visits.

Satisfaction

Approximately four out of five of the residents say that they feel satisfied. Some feel satisfied with their lives generally:

"Yes, my whole life! Basically, I'm very satisfied with most things."

"Just about everything in my life."

Some like having the necessities of life provided:

"Having a meal. Food is well prepared — nice dessert to look forward to — staff are pleasant."

"There's always enough good food; I can eat everything."

"I have a roof over my head."

"Everything is kept well and the food is good."

Others mention the quality of care they receive or the activities available in the care facility:

"The care I receive — the area I live in is nice to me."

"Having a good meal and watching TV."

"Yes, I'm satisfied. I was in a place and didn't like it one bit. It was like a hotel."

"Playing different games."

"Being provided for and comfortable."

"Satisfied with this good place and peace and quiet."

Some look forward to the future:

"Yes, thinking about family — health — I'm looking forward to a wedding."

"Bingo, TV, visits from friends."

"Being busy."

Some mention the way they are treated by others in the care facility:

"Nurses and care aides are all so nice."

"People are very nice — it's a nice, comfortable atmosphere."

"At my age, I should be [satisfied]. I have all I need . . . wonderful staff."

Others feel satisfied, but may have mixed feelings:

"My husband's happy — why shouldn't I be happy?"

"We have to be satisfied with what we've got."

"We have to accept things life gives us."

"I have to be here, so that's it. I can't look after myself at home, so I have no choice."

Some do not feel satisfied:

"I would prefer to be on my own."

"Not being able to do some work."

"It's not good being dissatisfied. That doesn't do anything — they just ignore it!"

"People don't do the job they're paid to do."

What friends, family, staff, and volunteers say about whether the residents are satisfied or not

More than two thirds of the family and friends interviewed, and almost all of the staff and volunteers, say that the residents with whom they are involved appear to be satisfied with life in the care facility. A few family and friends state that the residents are not satisfied with the variety of food in the care facility, with how safe their possessions are, or with their situation in general.

Sadness

One third of the residents say that they are often sad, frequently because a relative or friend has died. Some have ways of making themselves feel better when beginning to feel sad:

"There's no use feeling sad — that would just make it worse. I put it to the back of my mind."

"Adjusting to a different way of life takes time. I read."

"If someone dies, or loses something, that's the way it is — things change — get busy and do something."

"Sometimes when I don't feel well, I lie down and try to sleep."

"What's happening to Quebec — it's Canada. I read inspirational books, and they're a lot of help to me."

Some residents make an effort not to seem sad to others:

> "When in pain, I visit people and read the Bible."

> "I lost my daughter — I put on a smile."

> "I lost my brother recently — I get out of my room and mingle."

> "Every once in a while . . . why do I have to be in here? I work my way out of it myself. I don't talk to anyone about it."

A few residents often feel sad and say that they do not see a way to feel better, especially when they feel "dumped" or rejected by their families:

> "I feel forced into being here and would rather not be here."

At the other end, some say they never feel sad:

> "I've no one to feel sad about, and I don't care about anyone here."

What family, friends, staff, and volunteers say about the residents feeling sad

Unlike most of the questions asked in the research project, two out of five family and friends chose not to answer whether the residents with whom they are involved feel sad. Another two out of five say that the residents are not often sad. A few say that the person who feels sad didn't have a happy life or misses family and friends who have died, whether recently or many years ago.

In contrast to family and friends, almost all staff and volunteers feel that the residents are often sad. According to staff and volunteers, there can be a lot to be sad about:

- When residents first start living in the care facility, they miss homes, families, pets, and familiar things
- Some residents are struggling with loss of physical or mental abilities
- Some residents are sad when someone they knows dies in the care facility — and that is very common
- Over and over again, residents have to cope with changes and losses as table-mates or room-mates die or move to another part of the care facility and new residents take their places

Anger

Two thirds of the residents say that they do not get angry very often:

"I just go along with things."

"I feel frustrated because I can't use my legs."

"[There's] nothing to get angry about."

The third who often feel angry say that they do many things to overcome their feelings of anger. Some avoid the problem situation; some help others to see things differently; and some work their way through it:

"If other residents talk mad, fight, or swear, I come back to my room."

"Anything that goes wrong . . . I like things to run smoothly. I work my way through it myself."

"When I know I'm right and I don't get my way. They treat everyone the same way — and I want that to change. I work my way through it."

"When I have a fight with my relatives, I get busy."

"A lot of things. People being treated like that . . . I do something about it — teach them [other residents] to have some manners — to think of others!"

Some are angry only in certain situations:

"Not often — when someone bumps into me in the hall."

"Once in a blue moon — when other residents interfere when I'm visiting."

"A [resident] in the hall told me to stop walking around." (the person speaking is blind)

What family, friends, staff, and volunteers say about the residents being angry

More than four in five family and friends interviewed feel that the residents are seldom or never angry. Most of these family and friends say that what makes the residents angry is when people don't do what the residents expect, or when the residents cannot leave the facility or do what they used to physically, or when they have to have treatments that cause them pain.

In contrast to what the residents and their family and friends say, staff and volunteers feel that residents are often angry:

- with families, especially when they do not visit as often as the resident wants or do not visit at all
- with the staff when they do not want to do what the staff wants
- with other residents — for instance, when another resident is screaming.

Loneliness

Three quarters of the residents say that they do not feel lonely very often. Many add that there are reasons why they don't often feel lonely:

"I have people here."

"No, I don't think, so — I sometimes think of my family."

"No, because I read a lot."

"I've never been a lonely person — I keep my mind active."

"We all get lonely — that's just normal!"

"I'm quite happy — no time for feeling lonely."

The one in four residents who say that they often feel lonely explain that they miss their spouse or children. Or friends who no longer visit. In some cases the friend is not physically able to visit. In other instances, the friends are afraid to visit because they associate care facilities with hospitals, death, and dying.

Some residents say that they feel their loneliness is a result of how they have lived their lives:

"I brought it on myself for not having
   socialized more when I was younger."

   Although they may often feel lonely, some of
these residents have developed ways of making
themselves feel better:

"I say to myself, 'These damn people!'"

"I have conditioned myself with my reading."

"I go downstairs for a smoke."

"Once in a while, when I think of my son — I
   get out of my room."

"I go for a walk."

"I asked for the nuns to visit me and they did."

"I am lonely all the time — I lay back and go
   to sleep and forget about it."

   A few no longer try to feel better:

"I gave up on that."

What family, friends, staff, and volunteers say about the residents feeling lonely

Among family and friends, one third say that the residents often seem lonely. Staff and volunteers also say that many of the residents miss things they used to do and people they used to know. Staff and volunteers say that the residents who have few or no visitors or are involved in few of the facility's activities often seem lonely and isolated from others. Some add that the residents who cry or are depressed often feel better if hugged or talked with.

Part 1

Summary and suggestions

Part 1 shows that what might make a big difference to people who are socially isolated is to have their choices respected, whatever their choices may be. Whether you are a resident, family, friend, staff, or volunteer, there is something you can do now which might make a difference to the senior who is socially isolated. The checklists in this section contain many suggestions from the residents, family, friends, staff, and volunteers who participated in the research project. These are just some suggestions; each checklist has space for adding *your* ideas.

Summary of Part 1 Findings

One third of the seniors who participated in the research project say that they find it difficult mixing with other people in the care facility. Many spend a lot of their time on their own and may spend most or all of their time in their rooms. Many have few visitors. Many seniors mention that they have physical limits that affect their ability to socialize, and many also mention limits which have to do with personality and their ways of approaching life.

What this research project shows is that withdrawing from others is one way many of the residents cope with change. The senior who withdraws from others for a long or short time is often experiencing one or more of the following, and needs time and support to cope:

- has recently moved into a care facility
- did not plan to move into the care facility
- feels forced to live in the care facility by others
- had to move in suddenly
- prefers to be solitary and does not want change
- experienced a major change in health before moving into the care facility
- experienced a major change in health while living in the care facility
- has had several family members and friends die

SUGGESTIONS FOR WHAT YOU CAN DO TO ... make a difference to the senior who has just moved into the care facility

Ideas for Action:

Feeling Welcome
- Form a Welcome Committee of current residents to help new residents
- Start the welcome process before the person moves into the care facility (perhaps the Welcome Committee can visit, or send a greeting card, or send a list of things new residents might want to know)
- Encourage the Welcome Committee to try to support the new resident emotionally for the first month or months
- Ask staff for ideas about what would help the new resident

- _____

- _____

Knowing What's Going On
- Hang up an erasable slate or calendar where the person can easily see or reach it to write upcoming events important to the person and others — such as hair appointment, family visit, mealtimes, facility events
- Help the person find his or her way around the facility
- Post directional signs at eye level

■ Think about ways to make sure the resident's room is easy to find — for example, add easily identifiable symbols, an ornament or picture with a special meaning to the person, a flag or picture of the person's country of origin on the door

■ _____

■ _____

Who's Who
■ Ask the person whether she or he can read the nametags of staff and volunteers — should the print be larger?
■ Say your name aloud every time you meet a resident: "Good morning Mr. Jones. It's Martha, your nurse."
■ If the person seems to have difficulties seeing or remembering names, sensitively mention people's names as they approach
■ Ask the new resident what other ways you could help make names easier to remember

■ _____

■ _____

Understanding
■ Remember that most people need to withdraw from others for some time in order to cope with big changes in their lives
■ Respect the fact that withdrawing from others is not always something that has to be fixed

■ Remember that all residents will need time and support to find their way around, especially residents with physical or mental impairments

■ _____

■ _____

Offer Help
■ Ask the person what you can do to help
■ Give the person extra time and support
■ Check with the resident regularly to see whether she or he needs information repeated

■ _____

■ _____

Promote Independence and Respect
■ Lobby staff and management to relax the "rules" of the care facility for some time — for example, not insist that the person eat in the dining room or join in activities
■ Lobby staff and management to include ethnic dishes in the menu and to vary the menu using suggestions from residents
■ Find out about the Dignity of Risk (see Part 4) and how it is carried out in the care facility

■ _____

■ _____

Foster Positive Change
- Encourage residents and families to speak up if they have concerns
- Make sure that the new residents and their families know how to air their concerns
- From the very beginning, invite family members to be part of the Family Council (see next page), so that they feel connected to the care facility and what happens there
- Help make it possible for the Family Council to offer new residents and their families support through this transition period
- Make sure that the new resident knows about the Residents Council and what it does (see next page)

- _____
- _____

Residents Councils and Family Councils
Residents Councils differ in various facilities. In general, however, a Residents Council is a formally organized group of residents who inform management and staff about issues important to the residents in that care facility. The Residents Council helps staff and management know what types of activities the residents would like and what kinds of decisions the residents want to control.

A Family Council is a formally organized group of family and friends of residents. The Family Council meets regularly to encourage two-way comunication between the care facility and families, and works cooperatively to bring about change and resolve differences.

Residents Councils and Family Councils can identify, discuss, and present to the care facility administration suggestions on how to:
- increase the control the residents have over their lives
- review or revise rules and policies
- reduce some residents' feelings that change is impossible
- increase the residents' sense of involvement and belonging
- introduce new activities and interests

SUGGESTIONS FOR WHAT YOU CAN DO TO . . . make a difference to the senior who wants change, either to be left alone or to be more involved with people

Background Information:

Some seniors living in care facilities prefer to be solitary. For them, living among many other people may be difficult, especially at first. They do not want more contact with others. Some have been used to being alone for so long that they do not want to change. Some prefer being solitary to mixing with people they do not know. For many, the difficult part of living in a care facility is not wanting to be less solitary, but to have respect for their wishes to be solitary.

Other seniors want to be with people more. Sometimes they are shy, or have lost the social skills to start a conversation because they have been on their own for so long. Sometimes they try, and get rejected.

Ideas for Action:

Find Out What the Person Wants
- First and foremost, ask how the person feels about being around others and whether he or she wants change
- Develop a relationship with the person; discuss the things that generally interest him or her

- _____

- _____

Respecting the Senior Who Prefers to Remain Solitary

■ Be aware that the person's saying "no" to social activities may be just for today, or for every day, or just for this activity

■ If the person continually declines to join in social activities, ask whether she or he would prefer something else

■ Be aware that if sometimes your "help" isn't wanted, back off and don't pester the person

■ Remember that a person is not likely to become more sociable just because he or she lives in a care facility where there are many people

■ _____

■ _____

Monitor Your Own Behaviour and Reactions

■ Check whether you are respecting the senior's right to join in activities or to decline

■ Check whether you are labelling the person as "stubborn" or "antisocial" for not joining in — for instance, not wanting to eat in the dining room or play bingo

■ Check whether you or others are trying to force the person to do things

■ _____

■ _____

Helping the Senior Who Wants to Mix More with Others

- Ask about the person's life for special interests and tailor options to that
- Treat the resident as an individual; learn about the person's interests, hobbies and values — for instance, news, sewing, religion, language — which might help you introduce the person to others with similar interests
- Give the person extra time and support until things change for the better
- Look for opportunities for people to socialize one-to-one — make sure the person has chances to chat with a staff member or another resident
- Make sure that staff have opportunities to chat with residents without feeling they are jeopardizing their jobs
- If the person has lived in the care facility for more than a few months, ask her or him to join the Welcome Committee or be active on the Residents Council
- Make sure that the person knows about groups and activities which may interest him, or where she might find people with similar interests, and keep offering the information
- Ask the other people involved in the person's life — friends, family, other residents, staff, volunteers — for ideas that would make change happen
- Arrange a family conference with staff and compare ideas

■ If the person's major interest in life is smoking
and that is when he or she socializes, arrange
for an indoor smoking area or room if there is
none

■ _____

■ _____

SUGGESTIONS FOR WHAT YOU CAN DO TO . . . make a difference to the senior who is having difficulty adjusting to life in the care facility

- Help start an informal self-help group in the care facility.
- Find someone inside the care facility who can help — perhaps a recreation therapist, counsellor or social worker
- Find someone outside the care facility who can help — perhaps a counsellor or social worker
- Ask for ideas from the Family Council and the Residents Council
- Approach an advocacy group such as Advocates for Care Reform (see Helpful People in Appendix 2) for ideas or to work with the care facility management

- _____

- _____

SUGGESTIONS FOR WHAT YOU CAN DO TO ...
make a difference to the senior dealing with a lot of physical or emotional change and loss

Help the person adapt
- Ask the person what he or she needs to feel better
- Respect that the person may just want to watch activities without being forced to join in
- Make yourself available to the person for extra time and support
- Find out whether the person's situation is permanent or not — for example, will it be possible for the person to return home or not?
- Whatever the situation bothering the person, talk about it with her or him, even if only to let the person vent feelings
- Make sure that the person has a chance to sleep and be alone if that's what she or he needs
- Be aware that prolonged sadness may be a sign the person is seriously depressed, and may need medical help or grief counselling
- Ask the Recreation Therapist how activities can be adapted so that the person can participate

- _____

- _____

Remembering the Past
- Listen if the person wants to talk about his or her past
- Help the person remember the past — for example, find a wall, locker, or door in the person's room where she or he can display photos and paintings from home
- Listen if people want to talk about others who have died or about the fact that they are dying themselves and resist making suggestions about how the person could feel better

- _____

- _____

Respecting Losses
- Find ways to mark that someone else in the care facility has died
- Find out about any friendships with other residents who might be a comfort
- Don't try offering new connections until the person asks

- _____

- _____

Physical Connection
- Offer a gentle hug
- Find someone who could offer healing touch sessions for residents who want them

- _____

- _____

Planning for Change

■ Arrange ways for staff and volunteers to let the residents know when they are going to stop working at the care facility or change shifts

■ Talk with the person about ways to say good-bye to a favourite staff person or volunteer

■ If the person has to move from one care facility to another, involve the person wherever possible in choosing the facility, and discuss the change with the person in advance

■ _____

■ _____

SUGGESTIONS FOR WHAT YOU CAN DO TO . . . make a difference to the senior who wants more choice and control

Background Information:

This research project shows that there is a connection between seniors feeling socially isolated and being able to make daily decisions and have control over their lives. People who always have things done to or for them, and who have their choices made for them, may eventually lose the will and the capability to assert themselves. They may become passive and give up on trying to enjoy life. People with declining health or serious physical or mental impairments are most likely to have few choices in their daily lives in a care facility. Having control over their own lives and decisions affects how people look at themselves, affects how much they can cope with the inevitable changes in a care facility, and finally, affects whether they are willing to take chances with relationships with other people.

Family, staff, and volunteers often say that some residents like to have decisions made for them. This is particularly true for residents who have difficulty expressing their wishes. It is easy to slip into the pattern of making decisions for all the residents or even developing plans and programs, without asking the people involved.

The fixed routine of the care facility sometimes conflicts with what the residents want or need. Residents who have no control over whether they live in the care facility, and even those who planned to live in the care facility, want to feel that they have at least some degree of control over their lives. This includes taking time to withdraw from others if they wish.

Ideas for Action:

- First and foremost, ask the person before changes are made
- Plan ways so that the residents can have more say about the rules and policies of the facility — for example, ideas for changes to the menu could be placed in a suggestion box or given to the Residents Council

- _____

- _____

Flexibility in Routine

- Does she have to have meals at the same time every day?
- Can he "sleep in" if he chooses, even once in a while?
- Does she have a choice about what she eats?
- Can she choose her own table-mates and can she change table-mates easily and quickly?
- Can he eat alone in the dining room if he wishes?

- Can she choose whether she eats in her own room or in the dining room?
- Does he choose when to go to bed?
- Does she choose when to rest?
- Can he choose not to get up and eat at all, and have his choice respected?
- Does she choose what she wears?
- Does he have chances to buy or acquire new clothes?
- Do others ask permission before touching or moving her belongings?
- Do others respect his wish to be left alone?
- If she has physical impairments, is she ever forced to do what she does not want to do?

- _____

- _____

Part 2

What the residents and others say about meaningful relationships

VIGNETTE: Miss L., 72, lost all her work friends after her stroke, but then found what she calls "a wonderful new bunch" at the Adult Day Centre. Since moving into the care facility, however, she has no way to get back to the Centre. Her new friends aren't very mobile themselves, and can't come to visit her. Miss L. has been told that because the care facility provides similar activities as adult day care, they can't send her out to the Centre. She says she is alone in the world and feels depressed.

* * *

Introduction

As the vignette about Miss L. shows, meaning-ful relationships can be fostered or inadvertently undermined. In this example, Miss L. already had meaningful relationships with her friends at the Day Centre, but the rules and available funding effectively cut these relationships short. Encouraging more visitors and making more relationships possible for people who live in care facilities — two of the solutions most offered to reduce social isolation — are not as easy as they sound.

In Part 2, residents talk about various kinds of relationships — visits with family and friends, relationships with others, outlets for creativity and spiritual connections — and about what might be done to help people who seem lonely. Also included are brief looks at the perspectives of friends, family, staff, and volunteers. The section ends with a summary and checklists of suggestions for helping seniors in care facilities have meaningful relationships and keep in touch with others.

A. Visits with Family and Friends

Although spending time with family and friends is not a large part of a typical day for most of these residents, three in five say that family and friends are the most important thing in their lives.

For the majority of the residents, family and friends are their most regular visitors.

While one quarter of the residents say they have no visitors, or rarely have them, about one third of the residents say that they have regular visitors. A few residents receive visits daily. Some residents have several visitors who come by the care facility regularly.

More than half say that they have a visitor at least once a week and in many cases, more often. Seven out of ten of the residents have personal visits from people other than family and friends — for example, from a minister or a former co-worker. More than a third of these other people may visit weekly or even daily.

The residents spend their time with visitors in various ways, including listening to music, sharing a meal outside the care facility, studying the Bible, going to a movie or event, or going to a doctor's appointment. What many of the residents say they like most, however, is just talking with their visitors:

"Catch up on each other's news."

"Talk about old times — the good life."

"Much of it is about what the grandchildren are doing."

About one third of the residents note that having visitors in a care facility is harder than having visitors in private homes:

"We have to work around the mealtimes."

"Can't smoke [wherever we want]."

"There's hardly space for more than two people in my room. Lack of privacy."

On the other hand, a few of the residents find that visits at the care facility are easier than before:

"Everything is in one place."

"I'm usually at home!"

"This way, I don't have to provide refreshments."

"It's easy for them to come by car or bus, and there's enough parking."

About three in four of the residents meet their visitors in their room, which is also their bedroom. Many of the seniors find it socially difficult to entertain there, but it is the one room that is "home" to them and most under their own control.

In most intermediate care facilities and particularly in newer buildings, the residents have their own private rooms, and can entertain family and friends without others present. In extended care and in older buildings, however, sometimes two to four residents share a room, and it is very difficult to have a visit which is not interrupted by or shared with someone else — other residents, staff, volunteers, and even other visitors.

Whether in a private room or a shared one, many of the residents mention that the space can be cramped for people visiting:

"It's alright except when more than a couple of people, then there is no room."

"Not too much other place — so it has to be alright!"

The residents who have their own rooms say they like the privacy this allows during visits. Also, in the hustle and bustle of a care facility, closing the door of the room is sometimes the only way a resident who is hard-of-hearing can have a proper conversation with a visitor.

Some of the residents use the care facility's common areas for visiting, especially when more than one or two people visit at a time. Although it is possible in many care facilities for the residents and their visitors to book a space in the dining room or in the residents' kitchen, few of the residents mention that they eat a meal with their visitors in the care facility.

Most of the residents say that they are satisfied with the way their visits take place. A very few make suggestions for improvements to the visits:

"Get together socially only outside the care facility."

"I would like to serve tea or coffee in my room."

"It would be nice to have a private area for visits that's not in the room or in a public space."

"I'd like to have more visits."

What family, friends, staff, and volunteers say about visiting in general

Two thirds of the family and friends say that they visit the resident weekly or more often, while about one in five visit daily. The daily visits may be brief or last several hours.

Many of the family and friends comment that even though the care facility may welcome visits, they find it more difficult visiting in a care facility than in a private home. Like the residents, many mention the lack of privacy. Some deal with these problems by always having their visit with the resident outside the facility, either at a restaurant or at a private home. Some add that older friends and family don't like visiting any care facility.

In contrast to family and friends, most staff and volunteers feel that visiting in the facility is easy for visitors. They feel that difficulties have more to do with the families and residents than with the care facility. Most family and friends need time to adjust to visiting in the facility, and some never become comfortable. A care facility reminds some people of illness, hospitals, or death.

Family also often have other commitments to work or children. Staff say that even with extended visiting hours during the week, many families can visit only on weekends. As a result, the care facility may be crowded and noisy, and all residents and visitors are affected.

Staff and volunteers also say that few residents eat meals with their visitors, even though it is usually possible to arrange with a few hours' notice. Some family and friends mention that the prices charged for visitors' meals discourage them from eating at the care facility.

Only one third of the residents have regular visitors. Perhaps it is not surprising that staff and volunteers say that many family and friends do not visit residents often — or when they do, appear rushed and stay for just a short time. Many volunteers and staff feel that the residents whose family and friends seldom or never come to visit are generally more withdrawn than other residents.

What family, friends, staff, and volunteers say about visiting which is especially difficult

VIGNETTE: Mrs. S., 68, finds it painful when someone else in the care facility has a visitor. She breaks down and cries when she watches another resident's new grandchild being brought in to be admired. Her own baby died at birth and she says her husband never forgave her for the child's death. Her husband is dead, but Mrs. S. believes he is not visiting because of this event long ago.

* * *

Hurt feelings never heal in some families. About half of all families interviewed say that the most challenging difficulty in the visits is that there are unresolved issues between them and the resident. Some say that they never had a good relationship with the resident, and that is not likely to change. Others say that they do not visit long or often when the resident is angry or "negative."

Almost a third of the family and friends say that they find it difficult to visit because the resident has experienced a decline in physical or mental health. The resident may not be able to talk or talks with great difficulty, may be hard of hearing, or may tire easily and not be able to visit for long. The resident may have difficulty eating or swallowing, and may not want visitors there at mealtime. In some cases, the resident may have memory problems, and not remember the family's visit, or an outing, however recent. This resident may feel neglected — as though she or he was not visited at all. Some family and friends do not know how to keep a relationship with a resident going under these circumstances.

According to family, friends, staff, and volunteers, one other difficulty between the residents and family is that sometimes residents are very angry with their families for "dumping" them, as the residents put it, in the care facility. Visits under these circumstances may be tense for everyone.

Telephone and mail

Many residents keep in touch with others by telephone. Three out of four of the residents have telephones in their rooms and almost one third receive at least one phone call a day. Another third receive a call at least once a week. Many say that what they like most about having a telephone is keeping in touch with family and friends, both those who visit regularly and those who don't:

"To hear the person's voice."

"Hearing their concern for me."

"To keep abreast of the latest news."

"Mostly finding out what they're doing."

Fewer than one in five of the residents do not call or receive calls. Some do not have telephones. In many cases, these residents have difficulty speaking or are no longer able to use a telephone. In some cases, the resident prefers not to have a telephone or cannot afford to have it.

Almost half of the residents say that they receive very little or no mail, but those who do receive some like to read it over and over again. Many say that they don't write letters themselves — they may have physical impairments, or the mail service can't be counted on, or most of the people they used to correspond with have died, or it's easier to stay in touch by telephone.

B. Relationships with Others

About half of the residents say that they have one or more special relationships with staff or other residents:

"Just hit it off."

"Stopping to talk."

"Talking at mealtimes at our table."

"I go out of my way to keep on good terms
with everyone."

In care facilities, however, special relationships
with staff or other residents in care facilities can
end suddenly when a favourite staff member
leaves, or a resident-friend dies or must move to
a hospital or another care facility. Even residents
who have no special relationship with others in
the care facility say they see a constant coming
and going of residents and staff.

What family, friends, staff, and volunteers say about special relationships

Family and friends note that special
relationships do develop between residents or
between staff and residents who have spent
many years at the same care facility. Staff and
volunteers say that knowing the residents'
personal stories adds to the relationship they
have with those residents. Many staff and
volunteers say that they and the residents often
share information about each other's lives — for
instance, about children and grandchildren,
illness or good health, general family news.

Many staff say they would like to spend more
time talking with and getting to know residents in
a more personal way, but work-related
responsibilities prevent that. Staff also need to
balance respecting the person's privacy against
the fact that they need to know something about

the person to be able talk with them or to introduce them to others. Most staff say that they do not have enough time or resources to meet all the residents' needs.

Some staff also add that while they are expected to be impartial and "professional" with all residents, they develop a special feeling for some residents — for instance, those who are alone much of the time, whose family and friends do not visit, who have experienced a major change in mental or physical health, or who do not fit into the "mainstream" of the care facility — a much younger person in a care facility with many seniors, for example.

Help and support

The give-and-take of asking for and receiving help or support is one way that people can show they care about others and are cared about, and can be an important part of meaningful relationships.

In a care facility where there are many people with different abilities, there are also many chances for residents to help each other. One in four of the residents explain that they are not in a position to help others because of their own impairments. Some wait to be asked first before offering help. However, about one third say that they help other residents:

"I take a friend to her room — helping her
with her walker."

"I sometimes feed other residents."

"I can push others in their wheelchairs from
my wheelchair."

"I help my neighbour get back to her room
when she gets lost."

"I play music for them."

Three out of four of the residents say that they
do not mind asking others for help. Almost all,
however, say that they ask staff for help, not other
residents, volunteers, family or friends. About one
in four residents hesitate to ask anyone at all for
help:

"So long as I'm not overdoing it."

"Only in an emergency."

"People are awfully busy — everyone gets
angry."

"Depends who you're asking."

Some residents feel that family and friends are
not supportive, or say that they can take care of
their own affairs and do not need help. Three out
of four of the residents, however, feel that their

family and friends are very supportive, and welcome the various kinds of help. Some of the residents say that their family supports them by going to council meetings, looking after money and mail, or being the resident's advocate with the care facility staff and management.

Many of the residents mention the emotional support they receive:

"Anything I ask, they will do for me."

"By phoning every day."

"By listening to me and discussing things of interest."

"They bring gifts and remember my birthday."

"They show concern about how I'm doing."

What family, friends, staff, and volunteers say about help and support

Most family, friends, staff, and volunteers say that the residents with whom they are involved are willing to ask others for help. Staff say that they notice that many residents do not like to ask for help particularly during their first weeks in the care facility, and some never become comfortable asking for help.

Staff say that although the residents almost always ask staff rather than other residents for help, residents who are willing and able to help can make a difference to other residents. The resident may do such things as ask for help on behalf of another resident, help another resident use the telephone, or welcome new residents.

Three out of four family and friends say that they also help other residents. Many mention talking with the residents, or helping with wheelchairs, eating, and finding rooms.

According to staff and volunteers, about three in four of the residents have family and friends who support them in many ways — for instance, by taking them out shopping or to appointments, washing their clothes, bringing favourite food from home, or helping with facility activities.

On the other hand, staff say that some family and friends are not supportive. They do not consider the resident's need for financial or material support — they don't notice that the resident needs new clothing, for instance, or needs a haircut. Some family bring personal problems with them into the care facility. Some come to pay the resident's monthly bill, but never visit. Others appear only when the resident dies. Staff feel that the residents who are visited regularly are generally the ones who have families and friends who are most supportive.

Socializing outside the facility

Almost one third of the residents go outside the care facility at least once a day, alone or with others. The outing may be a walk around the building, a bus trip organized by the care facility, or a visit to the homes of family and friends. Most of the residents who go on outings feel satisfied with them:

"Would not be here without them."

"Love them."

"Look forward to them."

A few do not find the outings satisfying, and one reason may be declining health:

"Not very often — I fall too often to go out without a volunteer."

Some comment on the lack of fairness when it comes to who gets to go on outings, as well as the lack of control over where they go and how long they are gone.

Residents who go out least often may be those who cannot go out by themselves or do not have family and friends to take them. Few of the residents mention going out with volunteers or staff or other residents. Almost two of five residents say that they never go out, or leave the building very rarely.

In this research project, more than a third of the residents say that they spend six or more daytime hours (after getting up in the morning and before going to bed at night) alone in their rooms. Some of these residents are bedridden and some are "loners" who choose not to socialize with others, but many are alone for long periods of time and may be socially isolated.

According to the residents, most socializing inside the care facility (other than with family and friends) is planned by staff or happens by chance as a result of residents living in the same part of the building — for instance, meeting at the nursing station, gathering to smoke at the place designated for smokers, or talking with each other at mealtimes.

About half of the residents say that they are as socially active as other residents. One in five feel that they are more active than others. More than one third, however, feel that they are less active than other residents. About one in four meet with other residents in each other's rooms, but very few of the residents meet in groups not organized by staff. Those who do might watch a television program together in the common space, then discuss the program. Very few of the residents mention talking or doing activities with volunteers on an individual basis.

Most of the residents say that *any* activities help people who live in care facilities get to know one another, and that many activities are planned by staff. Activities mentioned include "happy hour," bus trips, Bible study, current events discussion groups, walks, and a monthly forum for people who are blind. One in five of the residents participate in such staff-planned activities:

"Go to all musical events."

"At mealtimes plus at bingo."

"In the afternoons and in the evenings, like to take part in everything that's going on."

Some go to the activities, but do not socialize:

"Pay attention to others and know what's going on, but don't talk to them — don't participate."

For about half the residents, mealtimes are when they spend the most time with others. For residents who stay in their rooms except for meals, mealtimes are the only time they are around people other than staff, family, and friends.

About one third of the residents say that mealtimes are not a time of socializing for them, however. Some are bedridden:

"Meals in room — have to be fed."

"All meals in bed."

Some don't like the hubbub of the dining room or don't have someone they want to talk with:

"Sometimes I don't go down [for meals] — I'm not much of an eater."

"There's lots of noise in the dining room — sitting with husband alone at a table."

"Sitting with people I don't get along with."

"I sit with people who wait for the last moment to show up at mealtimes."

"One friend [table-mate] died recently."

What family, friends, staff, and volunteers say about socializing

According to family and friends interviewed, about one third of the residents with whom they are involved get out of the care facility regularly, alone or with family and friends, to go shopping, or to a restaurant or library, or simply get out into the fresh air. Staff add that many residents also go to medical appointments, attend church, go out to have a haircut or a manicure, or join facility-organized bus trips. Most feel that the residents benefit from the outings by getting out of the care facility, and by being in touch with other people.

While staff and volunteers can clearly describe the activities possible for a resident, and the benefits, many say they don't know exactly how many residents never or rarely go out. Their estimates of residents who rarely or never leave the building vary widely, ranging from 1 to 80 percent. The average is about three to five out of every ten residents — close to what the residents themselves say.

Many staff and volunteers also say that they don't know how much time residents actually spend alone in their rooms — they estimate from two to three hours, to "a great deal of time alone," to "some loners never join in anything."

Family, friends, staff, and volunteers on the whole believe that there are many chances to socialize in a care facility — for instance, they notice ethnic groups sitting and talking together, the same group of residents always watching a certain television show, smokers gathering for a cigarette.

Most of the family, friends, staff, and volunteers feel that mealtimes are an important chance for the residents to socialize. Staff describe their efforts to seat people with similar likes or dislikes together, or to group those who need help eating or who disturb others. Staff also say that they receive many complaints from the residents that their table-mates have been changed or, where there has been a request, that they were not.

Some family and friends add that residents who have experienced a decline in health find it very difficult to socialize, however willing they might be. The resident may not speak clearly or may have trouble putting thoughts together.

C. Outlets for Creativity

Long-standing hobbies and interests can give residents a sense of continuity with their lives in the community, as well as a way to share common interests with others. Two out of three of the residents say that they still enjoy many of the hobbies and interests they had before they moved into the care facility. Some are solitary hobbies, while others put them in contact with other people:

"Playing the piano and accordion."

"Pussy cat, dogs, jigsaw puzzles."

"Fixing things."

"Crochet, jewellery, embroidery."

"Committee work and volunteer work."

Some make special mention of how the care facility supports their hobby or interest. Others say that they would like to pursue hobbies or interests, but are not doing so, mostly because their health has declined:

> "I sang in the church choir — I miss that, and also ballroom dancing."

> "I was a farmer and had no time for hobbies — now, I'm too old!"

> "My activities are restricted due to my sight."

> "Used to quilt — can't do it any more."

Almost one third of the residents say that they are interested in taking up new hobbies and interests, if given the chance. They also recognize that hobbies or interests may need to be adapted to meet their current physical abilities:

> "Woodworking, golfing."

> "Playing badminton."

> "Doing artwork, arranging flowers."

> "Folk dancing."

> "Being a writer."

"Doing volunteer work."

"Driving a car."

Some would like to see the care facility add to its programs:

"I used to weightlift — would like to do some."

"Facility doesn't support [my interest]. Just bingo!"

What family, friends, staff, and volunteers say about outlets for creativity

Over half the family and friends say that the resident with whom they are involved still has one or more hobbies and interests, but in many cases has changed what he or she does. For instance, a resident who loves bowling may be unable to lift regular bowling balls, but now uses big plastic bowling balls. A resident who used to play volleyball now watches it on television. A resident who used to crochet, sew, and make quilts now knits and spends more time reading.

Other family and friends say that some of the residents have given up former hobbies and interests, and are not taking up new ones. Once again, the reason is often that the person has experienced a decline in mental or physical health.

Most of the family and friends say that the care facilities offer programs which encourage the residents to continue with hobbies and interests. Somewhat surprisingly, even though many of these family and friends are in touch with the residents regularly, one third say that they do not know which hobbies and interests the resident would take up if she or he could.

Almost half of the family and friends say that physical impairments prevent the residents with whom they are involved from participating in hobbies and interests. About one in five also think that existing care facility programs do not make much difference to residents with physical impairments. A few add that programs are geared for hobbies that interest women more than men. Some family and friends would like to see the care facilities offer more — for instance, exercise programs, table games, reading material (for example, ethnic papers), and programs geared towards people who have visual or hearing impairments.

Many staff and volunteers mention that new programs often fall flat, as few or no residents participate, and that the greatest common interest of all residents is music.

D. Spiritual or Religious Connections

For many of the residents, keeping up their spiritual beliefs or religious faith helps them cope with changes in their lives, whether or not they have much contact with others or are experiencing major changes in health. Some say that a chance to enjoy music, art, or nature, and to feel that they are cared for and valued gives them a sense of meaning. Others want to attend church or to talk with others of their faith.

Two out of five of the residents say that they have opportunities to share their faith or religious beliefs with others. Some say that they discuss matters of faith with staff and other residents, while others say that they find it difficult because they cannot attend religious services. Almost one third of the residents either have no religious faith or spiritual beliefs or do not wish to communicate them to anyone.

What family, friends, staff, and volunteers say about faith and spiritual beliefs

Family and friends say that the residents go to church or attend chapel services, some to share their faith and others to socialize. Some of the residents do not have spiritual or religious connections because they have physical impairments or have never been religious.

Volunteers and staff, like many residents and family and friends, believe that having a religious leader such as a chaplain coming in to the care facility to hold services gives the residents chances to share their religious or spiritual beliefs. Bible studies are offered in some facilities.

E. People Who Are Lonely

What do the residents suggest can be done to help the one in four residents who feel lonely? About a third of the residents say they do not know what could or should be done to help:

"I don't know what people like — people can be very critical."

"I'm too busy myself to know the answer."

"I don't know what more could be done — maybe enquire more about what people like."

Some residents reject the suggestion that other residents could feel lonely:

"People here aren't lonely! There are plenty of outings."

"I don't know how they could be lonely!"

Others say that the person must take some responsibility for feeling lonely:

"They will have to make an effort to know more people."

"Residents should talk to others. Some just stay in their room."

"They have to come to terms with themselves."

"Teach them to have some manners — to think of others."

Some suggest a spiritual solution:

"Say a prayer, ask God for help."

"If people are really lonely — could something be done to bring God into their lives?"

One in four of the residents look towards the other residents and staff to spot and help the person who is lonely:

"Other residents should speak to these people and make them feel wanted and not alone."

"They need friends — people should trust everyone here as brothers and sisters."

"A staff person should talk to them."

"They [facility] should have a committee for welcoming new people."

"They [facility] should have more nurses."

"They [facility] should have the monthly meetings [where residents and staff discuss facility issues] more often."

"Have staff arrange more activities."

"Better care to help one enjoy the activities."

Some residents recommend more involvement by family, friends, and volunteers:

"If they have family — encourage their family to visit or phone."

"More visits by volunteers."

"We all feel that way! They should have more friends and visitors. Have a volunteer visitor."

Some of the residents stress making use of what is already there in the facility:

"Try and get them involved with activities — the aides are very thoughtful and good at helping."

"Some people would be happier if they could have a game of bridge."

"Get them into groups, out of their wheelchairs."

"Get into reading material."

"Attend the activities."

What family, friends, staff, and volunteers say about helping people who feel lonely

Like some of the residents above, some family and friends suggest that people who feel lonely take more responsibility for their situation. Some say that these residents need to "mix more," "make an effort," and "put themselves out." Others say that the residents need to be involved in more activities, especially crafts and exercise, and that ideally, to avoid becoming lonely, they would start such activities before moving into the care facility.

A third of the family and friends suggest that the resident who feels lonely would benefit from having a volunteer who would be with her or him one-on-one. Almost one in four of family and friends feel that more activities and entertainment, and particularly more appropriate ones, should be offered to the residents. Their suggestions focus on finding out what hobbies the residents truly enjoy and want, and on having more volunteers involved with the residents, especially ethnic volunteers. Another third recommend that family and friends keep in touch more often with the residents.

Staff and volunteers generally echo what family and friends say. They also think that family and friends should take the residents out of the care facility more often. They too suggest involving more volunteers, especially one-on-one with residents who feel lonely, and recruiting volunteers who speak languages other than English, as well as making more time for staff to spend with residents individually, and having seniors from the community and senior centres visit regularly.

Part 2

Summary and suggestions

Part 2 shows that many kinds of relationships are possible in care facilities. At the same time, some residents find it difficult to have or continue meaningful relationships — ones which include a sense of friendliness, trust, and understanding and caring about the other person. As a result, these residents may often feel "alone in a crowd."

Whether you are a resident, family, friend, staff, or volunteer, there is something you can do now which might make a difference to the senior who is socially isolated. The checklists which follow contain suggestions from the residents, family, friends, staff, and volunteers who participated in the research project. Each checklist also has space for *your* ideas.

Summary of Part 2 Findings

Looking at social isolation means looking at what relationships people say are possible and important to them. Most of the seniors find it possible and important to have relationships with at least a few other people. Some residents have very few relationships, and are content. Other residents have many relationships, and still feel socially isolated. Whether or not the relationships are meaningful may be a question only the individual senior can answer. Some residents who find relationships difficult may include:

- new residents, especially those whose move into the care facility is sudden or unplanned
- residents with declining health
- residents with physical or mental impairments
- residents who do not have telephones or cannot use them
- residents who do not speak or understand the language most others use in the care facility
- residents without family and friends or alienated from family and friends
- residents whose family and friends find it difficult to visit in the care facility

SUGGESTIONS FOR WHAT YOU CAN DO TO . . .
make a difference to the senior who finds visits difficult or unsatisfying

Background Information:

Family and friends are the most meaningful relationships many of the residents have — the residents usually trust their family and friends, and feel that they have the resident's best interests at heart.

About a third of the residents say that they have regular visitors, most of whom are family and friends. When the residents have satisfying relationships with visitors, they may care more about life, feel less socially isolated, and may cope better with change. In turn, visitors like to see the residents happy, well-adjusted and well cared for. Residents recognize that when they act "happy," visitors are likely to visit more often. Comments from both the residents and family and friends suggest that if a resident is too complaining or negative, visits will be cut short or not happen at all. That can be very hard for a resident who is sad or in pain.

Family visiting often drops off six months after the senior moves into a care facility. Family and friends may feel that because other residents and staff are around, the person is not isolated. Staff are usually busy with physical care, however, and have little time left for the other needs important to residents. Other residents may not be willing or physically able to "reach out." Many care facilities do not have enough volunteers, or do not see paying someone to coordinate volunteers as a priority.

Ideas for Action:

Focus on the Senior
- First and foremost, ask the person what would make a difference and see what change can happen
- Talk with the person about what is going on in her or his life and see what support she or he wants or needs

- _____

- _____

Respect Choices for Visiting
- Talk with the person about whether she likes to have visitors (who, when, and for how long)
- Ask the person when he usually feels most like socializing and try to visit then
- Ask recreation staff to make a sign for the person's room — for example, "I have company. Please do not disturb." or "I'm resting. Please come back in half an hour."
- Find ways to involve volunteers in visiting the resident who has few or no family and friends, but ask the resident first

- _____

- _____

Accept the Person "As Is"

■ Find a way to accept that the person is changing — for instance, his health may be declining and he may need family and friends to talk about these changes as well as adjust their visits to these changes

■ Expect that like anyone else, the person will have "good" days and "bad" days, physically and emotionally, and will not feel the same every visit

■ _____

■ _____

Making Visits Pleasurable

■ Make sure that you are doing what the person enjoys and not what you think the person should enjoy or only what you enjoy

■ Be aware that most residents enjoy just spending time with visitors, and do not always want or need activities

■ Take the time for visits, and do not treat it as just another chore or obligation

■ Find ways to use space in the care facility so that residents and visitors can have privacy at least sometimes

■ Even if the person likes large groups of visitors, make time to visit alone too

■ Let the person know that he or she still gives you and others caring and support

■ Ask whether the person would like to share a home-cooked meal of favourite foods with you

■ Ask the person whether there is a favourite
  food you could bring

■ _____

■ _____

Connections with Others

■ Remember that there are many ways to keep in
  touch with people in addition to visiting —
  including telephone and letters
■ If the person wants to use the telephone to stay
  in touch with others, find ways to make it
  possible
■ Be aware that residents who receive mail like
  to read it over and over again, and that it may
  be an important link for people with failing
  memory or with faraway family and friends
■ Ask about reading mail or writing letters for the
  person
■ If the person you are visiting agrees, include
  another resident in your visit sometimes

■ _____

■ _____

Respecting Spiritual Needs

■ Be aware that some seniors may want to talk
  about and share their faith or spiritual beliefs
■ Be aware that some seniors may want to talk
  about death, and may not have any opportunity
■ Find ways in addition to attending church or
  inviting a chaplain for seniors who choose to

talk about and share their faith or spiritual
beliefs with others

■ _____

■ _____

Planning
■ If visiting hours in the care facility are not
flexible, find out how to change them
■ Communicate with other family and friends so
that everyone doesn't visit the resident at the
same time
■ If there are family and friends with jobs and
children who must visit on weekends, ask
family and friends who can be more flexible to
visit during the week instead
■ Plan for making it possible for a family member
or friend to stay overnight when the resident is
ill
■ Only if the person chooses, arrange to share a
meal at the care facility — in the dining room or
in the person's room, as he or she likes

■ _____

■ _____

SUGGESTIONS FOR WHAT YOU CAN DO TO . . . make a difference to the senior on an outing from the care facility

Background Information:

What many of the seniors say is that next to visits with family and friends, they most enjoy getting out of the care facility. What is true, however, is that many of the seniors never or rarely leave their rooms or the care facility, and more than a third often spend six or more daytime hours alone in their rooms.

Ideas for Action:

Family and Outings
- Find out what interests the person has and find out what he or she wants to do
- Be aware that outings may be as simple as going for a walk down the hall or around the outside of the care facility
- Pick up a calendar of activities from recreation staff
- Be aware that outings the residents say they like are not limited to medical appointments, church, or facility-organized bus trips, but include visits to the homes of family and friends, going shopping, or for a drive, or to a restaurant or library
- If family or friends are not from nearby, they may not know what activities are going on in

the community — keep handy a list of places to go and places to eat
- If the person agrees, include another resident on a family outing
- Be aware that because there are often not enough volunteers, seniors who need help walking or moving or who have few or no family and friends may rarely get out of their rooms or out of the care facility

- _____

- _____

Facility-Sponsored Outings
- Make sure that the residents, their family and friends know when facility-organized outings are taking place
- Get to know the recreation staff and remind them to include the person in outings
- Ask the person what makes it hard for him or her to go out, and find out what change is possible — for instance, the resident may need someone to go with her or him
- Keep a log of which residents go on outings and find out whether residents who never go on outings would like to be included
- Have one or two residents survey other residents on the kinds of outings they would like to have
- Ask seniors who have physical or mental disabilities what would make it possible for them to go on outings, if they want to

- Ask family and friends to accompany the resident on bus outings as a companion or as a volunteer
- Plan ways to involve family and friends in outings more often — for instance, have an outing for a weekend afternoon when they may not have to work

■ _____

■ _____

SUGGESTIONS FOR WHAT YOU CAN DO TO . . . make a difference to family and friends who find visits difficult

Background Information:

While extending visiting hours is something many care facilities do to encourage visits, many of the seniors and their family and friends say that visiting is difficult in care facilities and that there are things that can be done to make visits better for everyone.

Ideas for Action:

- Make sure that family and friends have information about visits — for example, when the resident prefers visitors; how to share a meal if the resident agrees; time of meals if the resident does not want visitors then; where and how to get a cup of tea or a snack
- Find out how to make visiting possible more often for a family member or friend who cannot drive, take transit, or afford cabs
- Find ways for family and friends to share more meals with the person — where, when, and if the resident chooses
- Make sure that family and friends know if there is a residents' kitchen which can be booked by residents or their families and friends to do their own cooking and have a private group meal, birthday party, or other event

- Use common space in the care facility —
  including the dining room, which is often empty
  for part of the day — to make spaces for
  people to visit outside the residents' rooms
- Especially in extended care facilities, look at
  what can be done to make halls and rooms
  less hospital-like and more welcoming to all
  visitors
- Find ways to make small children welcome and
  occupied — perhaps a toy box in the lobby
  where the child can choose a toy or game to
  play with while visiting, and books or games for
  older children
- Keep a Visitor Log or Guest Book on the
  resident's wall or door and ask visitors to sign it
  or add a few comments; this may help the
  resident remember that someone was there
  and make the visitor feel special
- Arrange special evenings for residents and
  their family and friends, and put up posters in
  the facility well in advance, using themes such
  as Valentine's Day, Mother's Day, Father's Day,
  St. Patrick's Day, Robert Burns Day, or
  planning around seasons — a strawberry tea,
  summer barbecue, or picnic
- Make sure that family and friends know that
  they are welcome and needed on the Family
  Council or the Residents Council if there is one

- _____
- _____

SUGGESTIONS FOR WHAT YOU CAN DO TO . . . make a difference to the senior who finds starting or keeping meaningful relationships difficult

Background Information:

Many relationships are possible and important in a care facility, and the resident is the best judge of whether or not they are meaningful. In general, meaningful relationships often include give-and-take, with the person being able to offer and be valued for help, as well as being able to receive help and support. Meaningful relationships also often involve having outlets for creativity and spiritual connections.

Ideas for Action:

Respecting the Person and Personal Choice
- Respect the person's feelings as real — for instance, the senior who has few or no family and friends or who cannot remember visitors may always feel sad when she sees that others have visitors; instead of telling the person to "cheer up," offer some time to spend together
- Find out from the person what other residents or volunteers can do to help make his life better
- Find out what skills or life experience the person may be able to offer to others if she chooses
- Lobby for support from management for making money and space available for the

residents' non-physical needs — emotional, spiritual, creativity, relationships
- Be aware that many new residents hesitate to ask anyone for help or information — you may have to take the initiative and offer it
- Lobby management for changes to mealtimes — many residents say that they want to sit where and with whom they choose instead of having to sit in the same place and with the same people every day

- _____

- _____

Respecting Relationships
- Keep in mind that even seniors who prefer to be alone have at least a few relationships, and these relationships may be especially meaningful and important to them
- Keep in mind that most residents care about someone, and sometimes have very special relationships with other residents, staff, and volunteers
- Respect the person's right to know when other residents, staff, or volunteers move, leave, or die
- Ask the resident about a person who has died or left the facility and listen if she needs to talk about the person
- Find ways for the person to visit or stay with a sick friend in the care facility

- _____

- _____

Feelings and Spiritual Issues

■ Be aware that most staff have to focus their limited time and energy first on the residents' physical wellbeing, then on their emotional or spiritual wellbeing

■ Be aware that family, friends, staff, volunteers and other residents sometimes inadvertently discourage the person from talking about death and dying

■ Be aware that many seniors need frequent chances to talk about their feelings and to look back on their lives, even if they do not choose to talk at one particular time

■ Be aware that some seniors need chances to talk about spiritual issues

■ Be aware that for some residents, having a chance to enjoy music, art, or nature, and to feel that they are cared for and valued gives them a sense of meaning more than going to church or talking about religious beliefs

■ Be aware that some residents need to talk with others of their faith, especially if they can no longer attend church

■ Explore ways to involve volunteers from churches and spiritual groups in helping residents talk about and keep in touch with their spiritual beliefs or religious faith

■ _____

■ _____

Keeping Active or Involved

- Be aware that the purpose of activities is not simply for the person to be active, but for the person to enjoy, have fun, and be pleasantly distracted
- Make sure that all residents can easily find out what activities and events are going on in the care facility
- Be aware that many of the seniors, whatever their impairments, can and do help others
- Find out whether the person wants to help others in some way
- Explore the possibility of setting up an intergenerational program in the facility (see Helpful People in Appendix 2)
- Be aware that many residents like music, even though their taste in music may vary
- Be aware that many residents do not stop having ideas for new hobbies and interests just because they have moved into a care facility or have experienced a decline in health
- Find out what interests and hobbies the person has now and find out what he or she still wants to do
- Make sure that the activities offered match the person's abilities, adapting the activities where necessary
- Ask the person what is preventing her or him from doing a favorite hobby or interest, and find out what change is possible — for instance, she may need tools to work in the garden, or have flower beds at waist height; he may need

someone to show him a new skill, or may need
money or help to buy supplies
- Ask family and friends to donate tools (or
materials, games, puzzles) or organize a
fundraising to buy some
- Explore ways to increase the number of trained
and supervised volunteers in the care facility,
including how to keep them involved and
rewarded (see the last checklist in this section)

- _____

- _____

Respect Differences
- Offer some activities geared specifically to men
or specifically to women
- Encourage more males to volunteer with male
residents
- Find out what activity programs especially
interest residents who would like to be more in
contact with others — for instance, exercise
programs, table games
- Make sure that there is a wide variety of
reading material — for instance, non-English
papers, large print, talking books

- _____

- _____

Respect Changing Health and Capabilities

- Look at ways of having the public library talking books or large print book service come to the facility
- Lobby management for programs geared towards people who have visual or hearing disabilities
- Look at ways of adapting existing programs to meet the changing needs and abilities of the residents

■ _____

■ _____

SUGGESTIONS FOR WHAT YOU CAN DO TO . . . make a difference to the senior who feels lonely

Background Information:

In general, the suggestions from the residents, family, friends, staff, and volunteers to help people who feel lonely in the care facility focus on the following:

- one-on-one relationships
- stimulation
- lots of visits from family and friends
- activities that interest the person
- frequent outings of interest to the person
- more support for ethnic diversity
- more volunteers needed

The following ideas for action focus on the seniors who feel lonely. Since so many people in the research project suggest that volunteers might make a difference to seniors who feel lonely, a separate section follows of background information and ideas about volunteers in a care facility.

Ideas for Action:

- Find out what hobbies the person has or would like to do
- Take the senior out as often as possible

- Remember special occasions with visits, calls, cards, flowers, treats, gifts
- Visit or phone as often as you can
- Keep the person informed about what's happening in the family or in the care facility
- Bring photos to look at with the person
- Tell the person what you like about him or her
- Bring newspapers or other material in the person's language
- Recruit more volunteers, especially ethnic volunteers for seniors of the same background
- Offer the senior with few or no family and friends regular times of undivided attention with the same volunteer
- Find out whether the person would like someone to read to him or her; or whether a group of people would like to hear a book together
- Find out whether the person would like to choose and watch a video movie with someone else
- Have a pet day when family or volunteers take a gentle pet in to visit
- Invite seniors from the community and seniors' centres to visit and become more involved — not only as volunteers, but also as people who might be interested in some of the programs and activities

- _____
- _____

SUGGESTIONS FOR WHAT YOU CAN DO TO . . . make a difference to volunteers in a care facility

Background Information:

Most staff say that there are limits to how much time they can spend talking with and getting to know the seniors in a more personal way. Most staff must focus their time and resources on physical care, and do not have enough time or resources to meet all the seniors' other needs for help, support, information, time, undivided attention, outlets for creativity and spiritual or religious beliefs.

One of the most common suggestions of residents, staff, family and friends is to use more volunteers in care facilities. Volunteer involvement, however, can be more challenging than most people realize. Compared to five or ten years ago, many more volunteers are students or new immigrants; a significant number have English as their second language; and many only have a short-term commitment to volunteering. Volunteers today often need more supervision that in the past. Long-term committed volunteers with experience are often stretched to the point of exhaustion, and eventually give up volunteer work.

Volunteers can be family and friends or other people who want to help. Volunteers who can stay longer — for instance, more than a year — are especially needed to help reduce the number of new people with whom residents have to cope. There are many ways to encourage volunteers to keep giving time and energy to the residents of care facilities.

Ideas for Action:

Recruiting
- Remember that sometimes the most dedicated volunteers start off as family or friends and then move into volunteering after the death of the resident
- Let family and friends know that they are appreciated as visitors and volunteers, even after the resident they are involved with dies
- Lobby management for a trained and paid Volunteer Coordinator who will recruit, train, plan, and supervise programs that use volunteers effectively
- See if there is a Volunteer Bureau in your community and contact them for ideas and help (see Helpful People in Appendix 2)
- Recognize and work with the fact that some volunteering is going to be for a short time and be limited to the volunteer's individual goals or interests — for instance, learning English, getting skills and experience before applying for a paid job

■ Recruit volunteers who have training and experience with specific groups, such as the Alzheimer Society

■ _____

■ _____

Training

■ Provide volunteers with a specific job description, including expectations about time to be devoted
■ Make sure the volunteers are trained on how to best assist people with impairments
■ Offer volunteers a wide variety of experiences based on their skills or interests — for instance, someone who likes to read could read to a resident; someone whose paid work involves conflict resolution or counselling could facilitate disputes between residents, or residents and family
■ Make every effort to match the resident with the volunteer

■ _____

■ _____

Show Appreciation
- Plan ways to let volunteers know they are welcome and appreciated — for instance, a volunteer appreciation tea or other event; certificates for service; letters of reference for volunteers upgrading their résumés

■ _____

■ _____

Part 3

Extra challenges

Introduction

Part 3 looks at the extra challenges some residents face in coping with change and in having or continuing relationships. While all of the residents who participated in the research project are cognitively able and willing, many are coping with one or more conditions which they say greatly affect their ability to have relationships with others.

This section summarizes what the residents, friends, family, staff, and volunteers say about extra challenges to getting around the care facility or mixing with other people. The section ends with a checklist of suggestions for what might make a difference to these people who face more obstacles than most who live in care facilities and are very likely to be socially isolated.

A. Physical Impairments

Mobility impairments

A mobility impairment is a condition that makes the resident's ability to move around difficult or impossible without the help of someone else. More than half of the residents in this research project have a major mobility impairment. Some may use a walker or a wheelchair to move around as they choose — get together with others if they wish, move around the building, or participate in activities. Others may have a wheelchair or a walker, but still may not be able to get around easily — for instance, they may have little upper arm strength and need help from others to go anywhere. Some may have one or more other conditions in addition to the mobility impairment — such as impaired vision or the results of a stroke. This last group of residents may find it extremely difficult to get together with others or to participate in activities.

Many residents say that their physical impairments greatly affect their ability to socialize, mix, or do things. Three out of five family members and friends also identify physical conditions which make it difficult for the resident with whom they are involved to get around and affects her or his ability to mix with others and to do things. The impairment can affect the person from day to day or hour to hour. For instance, on one day, the person with arthritis may be able to enjoy a visit with family and eat in the dining room. On the next, the person may be in excruciating pain, find the company of other people unbearable, and may be unable to leave her or his bed.

In stark contrast to what the residents and their family and friends say, most staff and volunteers in this project feel that physical impairments do not significantly affect the ability of residents to mix with others or to do things. Many staff and volunteers seem to feel that because they bring the residents to the activities, the difficulty is overcome.

For many of the residents, physical difficulties are not overcome by having someone wheel them everywhere. Others may not always be there when the resident wants to move. The resident may spend much time waiting for someone to help. Others may move the resident without asking whether or where the resident wants to go. Others may move the resident when it is convenient for them, rather than for the resident. Some residents get tired of asking family, staff, or another resident for help, and give up trying to go anywhere. Some feel that they are constantly imposing on others, or feel that they

can't possibly repay such favours — and they too
give up.

Visual impairments

VIGNETTE: John has had diabetes for most of
his life. He developed glaucoma three years ago
and has very little eyesight remaining. Six months
ago he moved into the care facility. He's met a
charming lady whom he'd like to get to know
better (he ran right into her), but now he can't find
her!

* * *

Over one half of the residents say that they
have difficulties seeing and that this greatly
reduces their socializing and their participation in
other activities. Some residents with difficulties
seeing have macular degeneration, cataracts, or
glaucoma. They are very sensitive to the fact that
their eyesight is declining, and are very aware
that less vision may mean that they will not be
able to enjoy their lives as much.

The group of residents who participated in the
research project has more than double the level
of visual impairments that is considered the
"norm" for incoming residents. It may be that
health care assessments are not catching
people's difficulties seeing before they are
admitted to the care facility. Or the residents'

vision may undergo rapid changes while they are living in a care facility. Both are possible.

Many residents who are blind or who have visual impairments say that others often bump into them. Some stay in their rooms where they feel safe. When they do come out, they often do not socialize much because they cannot see people clearly or at all.

Residents who are blind or who have visual impairments say that it is extremely difficult for them to find others in the care facility. Whether the person has been blind or visually impaired from birth, early in life, or later in life, she or he has unique problems. Residents with vision impairments say that one thing that would make a difference to them is if people would announce their presence — for instance, "Hi, John. It's Martha here." Another is being considerate — for example, offering an arm for the resident to take, not grabbing the resident's arm.

People who are blind or who have visual impairments say that they often feel blamed by others if they don't socialize much. Staff, volunteers, family, friends, and other residents may tell the person to take more initiative, or to mix more. Such comments often push the person deeper into isolation because, even with effort, the person can only do so much on her or his own. She or he needs the help of staff, volunteers, and especially family and friends, over and over again.

Again, as with mobility impairments, staff and volunteers may not be aware of the impact visual impairment has on the lives of residents. Some staff and volunteers mention that residents with visual impairments can still play musical instruments. Some mention that the care facility has specially designed hand-rails to help residents with sight impairments find their way along halls. Some erroneously believe that other senses, such as hearing, may take over and make up for the sight impairment. Many staff and volunteers say that they have not been adequately trained about how to work with people who are blind or visually impaired.

Hearing impairments

VIGNETTE: Her friends know her as Harriet, and she asks that the staff call her Mrs. H. She is 91 years old. She is blind and hard of hearing. Three months ago, her best friend moved to another facility. Mrs. H. says she lacks the energy to try to start another friendship. She rarely leaves her room, and says it has been three days since she last talked with someone.

✻ ✻ ✻

More than two thirds of the residents have hearing impairments that they say make socializing and doing certain activities difficult or impossible. Like Mrs. H., they may give up trying to have relationships with others.

Many people with hearing impairments use hearing devices. As with people with mobility impairments, devices don't solve problems for everyone. Most hearing aids simply amplify sound. For many people this doesn't help the problem — in fact, in a care facility which is noisy, a hearing aid may pick up so much noise that it makes the situation worse.

The residents say that sometimes people who have hearing impairments are thought to be "confused" or suffering from dementia. Other people's words may not make sense to them and their actions may not match what someone else is asking or saying. They may often show that they are frustrated and angry.

One half of the family and friends are aware that many residents have hearing impairments. Family and friends say that some residents do not hear exactly what is said, and may become irritable and avoid groups. For many residents, the difficulty gets worse as they get older. The remainder of family and friends either are not aware of the resident's hearing impairment or are not aware of the extent of the difficulty the resident has hearing.

Staff and volunteers say that many residents who have hearing impairments or who are deaf appear to be in difficult circumstances, if only because they have so little social interaction. Other residents tire of trying to make themselves understood, and the people with hearing impairments become tired of the effort of asking others to speak up, to face them so that they can figure out what is being said, to repeat or rephrase things, and not to "mumble." For people who have severe hearing impairment, using the telephone — that social link so important to many other residents — has become impossible.

Some staff and volunteers say that they find residents who have hearing impairments a strain and difficult to relate to. Many staff and volunteers also say that they have not been adequately trained about how to talk with people who are deaf or hearing impaired.

Pain and low energy

VIGNETTE: Mrs. M., 77, has no problems with her vision and hearing, but for years has had osteoporosis and failing kidneys, along with a few other serious physical conditions. Despite this, she managed to work as a registered nurse until she was 70.

She lived in her own apartment with the occasional help of a homecare aide. Making meals and even dialling the telephone to talk with her children became a huge physical effort on days when her energy was especially low. Although she had kept up with a circle of family and nursing friends for many years, she gradually withdrew so that her world was mostly the television and her living room sofa.

Then she fell and broke her hip. After two days of waiting for someone to show up, and a two-month stay in the hospital, she was moved into the care facility without ever going home again. She cannot move or walk on her own, even with a walker. Sitting in bed or in a wheelchair is painful. She feels depressed sometimes and often says she doesn't have the energy to deal with people any more. After a few months of staff and family trying to persuade her to eat in the dining room and go to activities, she now spends all of her time in bed watching television, eating meals, or sleeping, just as she did in her own home. "I want to see all the TV programs I missed while I was working all those years," she says.

* * *

Like Mrs. M., many people with physical and mental impairments have very low energy and may be in constant or frequent pain. Over half of the residents say that they are suffering from low energy that hinders their socializing and their participation in activities. The rest say that they usually have enough energy to do some things, if they pace themselves.

Family and friends say that some times are harder than others for the residents with low energy. Some conditions — like diabetes, for instance — are not always under control, and the person becomes weak and has no energy left for socializing. Medication may make the person groggy or disoriented. Sometimes the person feels depressed and lacks the will to be mobile. Sometimes the person finds it so complicated to go out, and so difficult to keep up with others, that he or she gives up going on outings of any kind. The person may still have "good" days when more is possible — for instance, when there is enough energy to be wheeled to and from the hairdresser's salon, and to sit up in the hairdresser's chair for half an hour for a haircut. The person may spend the rest of the day exhausted after such an outing.

Residents who have low energy may not appear to have any impairment. As a result, others may expect them to "try harder" when they may already be trying as hard as they can. For example, some staff and volunteers interviewed say that they find residents who have low energy "passive" — like Mrs. M., many stay in their rooms and sleep a lot. Some staff say that they try to coax these residents out, but that they are "harder to motivate."

Many of the residents suffer chronic pain from such conditions as osteoporosis, rheumatoid arthritis, and osteoarthritis. Some doctors do not prescribe strong pain medication. As a result, the pain of some seniors is never or rarely under control. Almost half of the residents say that the pain they suffer is severe enough to hinder them from moving around, mixing with others, or doing things:

> "I'm more comfortable when sitting in special recliner."
>
> "When it's painful, [I get] cranky."
>
> "I get very uncomfortable — and am sometimes quite groggy — on morphine."
>
> "When I have very strong pain, I feel like staying in my room."

Family and friends interviewed are not always as aware of the pain which over half of the residents suffer. Fewer than two out of five family and friends say chronic pain makes it difficult for residents to interact with others or to do things. Some residents who talk often about their pain are seen as "constant complainers." As the comments of the residents, staff, family, and friends about visiting show in Part 2, chances are better that a resident will have visitors if the resident does not talk often about "negative" aspects of his or her situation. Like residents with other kinds of impairments, the resident who has chronic pain has the extra challenge of balancing her or his need to talk about how he or she is feeling, with how much family and friends can stand to hear.

Cognitive impairments

By necessity, this research project did not include interviews with residents who have major cognitive impairment; however, some family members interviewed spoke on behalf of residents who have cognitive impairments.

People who have cognitive impairments may forget names, even of close family members. They may have trouble finding the right noun or verb. They may ask questions over and over again. They may not be able to string ideas together, and may easily lose their train of thought. They may finally stop trying to talk because it's so much effort or because they don't want to make a mistake or look foolish. (For valuable understanding of people with cognitive impairments, see Moyra Jones' *Gentlecare* in Appendix 2, Helpful Reading.)

Some of the residents in the research project talked about how they feel about living with people who have cognitive impairments. Their answers show that many people with cognitive impairments may be left alone by other residents, and may easily become socially isolated:

"Useless to mix — not many are sharp."

"I think they're mostly senile — waste of time to have a discussion with them."

Other conditions

More than one third of the residents say that they experience other conditions which they feel isolate them from others and from activities in the care facility. Some residents have had strokes. They can find it very difficult to speak or to be understood by others, and they withdraw. Other residents withdraw because they have a condition they find embarrassing — such as being incontinent, having to wheel an oxygen tank around with them, using a cane or walker, having tremors, or choking on food. Some who are losing their memory do not want others to know.

B. Economic Circumstances

Like most people everywhere, people who live in care facilities sometimes worry about money, and find that lack of money affects what they can do and how they can connect with others. The only source of income many seniors have is Old

Age Security and the Guaranteed Income Supplement. Because the cost of care is high — compared to what these seniors have — there may be little left over to pay for things like a telephone, cable service, new knitting needles, newspaper subscription, a few plants, a magazine, lunch on outings, having hair cut or styled, buying new clothing. For residents with this kind of economic reality, staying connected with the outside world is a dream.

Some families have low incomes. These families may not be able to visit as often as they and the resident would like because they cannot afford extra travel costs, whether by car, bus, train, or ferry. Some may not be able to afford to pay for a meal with the resident in the care facility. Families with young children may not be able to afford regular babysitters or child care, and may want to bring the children with them to visit.

While some residents in the research project still control their own finances, others have money that is administered by family. In some cases, the arrangement works well, especially where the family and the resident have worked out ways of doing things so that the resident is comfortable and has bills paid without question.

Sometimes, however, the arrangement does not give the resident peace of mind. The resident may be placed in the uncomfortable position of having to ask for an "allowance." The resident's family may refuse to make money available, even though it is the resident's money, and the resident may suffer as much as someone who has no money to spare. Residents who do not control their own money may never be sure whether there is enough. They may worry that their money will run out, that their families will not be able or willing to make up the difference, and that they will have to make even more changes.

C. Language

While communicating with others does not depend only on being able to talk, talking is often the first way most people try to communicate. Residents who do not understand or speak the language of those around them are very likely to be socially isolated. Some never learned the language. Some return to their mother tongue. Others forget the "new" language or simply feel more at ease with the language that is familiar to them.

If most of the staff in a care facility speaks only English, a resident who does not may only be able to communicate when family and friends come to visit and can translate. The rest of the time, this person may withdraw from others and have great difficulty finding her or his way around. In turn, some residents who speak English only say that they have difficulty communicating with staff and volunteers who are learning to speak

English or do not speak it very well yet or feel shy
with their command of the language.

D. The Building

Many of the residents say that they found it
difficult at first adjusting to their new surroundings
in the care facility. It can easily take residents a
few weeks to several months to adjust. A few
never do.

Most residents who have lived for some
months in their new home say that they can find
their way around the care facility. Many residents
add, however, that the sheer size of the building
makes getting around or socializing difficult.
Compared to most private homes, the distances
are large. To get to the dining room, or other
location important to them in the building, many
residents in care facilities need to walk or
otherwise move the equivalent of a city block to
go from their room to the dining room or other
location important to them.

For people who have impairments, long
distances are often difficult. Just getting around
the building may take considerable time and
energy. Residents with physical impairments of
any kind often find it difficult to navigate through
large numbers of constantly changing and
moving people and objects. The person trying to
move a wheelchair finds that other people may

move quickly, or very slowly, and often unpredictably. The person who has a hearing impairment finds that he is distracted and confused by several conversations going on at once in the dining room and the loud blend of television and radio programs filling the hall. The person who is blind finds that someone has moved or rearranged furniture in the lounge and that there are several linen and medication carts in the hall.

Many residents who have impairments say that they do not like to ask often for directions or help. Some say that after the first few weeks of being in the new care facility, people are less patient and helpful, and that residents who keep asking for help or directions may be suspected of having dementia. Some residents begin to feel responsible for not being able to find their way:

| "I'm blind — so I didn't ask questions." |

A building which is laid out with the residents — especially the many residents who have impairments — in mind can make it much easier for new residents to step out and try new things and perhaps make new friendships. Building design can also make a difference to how satisfying visits are for the residents and their visitors. Some residents who have lived in more than one care facility say they prefer the smaller, more intimate size of some care facilities, although these smaller facilities may offer fewer activity programs.

Signs are often introduced into a building as an afterthought. While they provide help to some residents and visitors, they do not help the person who is blind or has a visual impairment. These residents say that buildings with large open spaces and rooms and hallways with non-traditional angles (other than 90-degree standard corners) are also a major problem to orientation.

Most family and friends say that they find it relatively easy to find their way around the care facility once they have been there a few times. Staff and volunteers say that when they first started working in the care facility, they had to take time to learn their way around. Many staff had suggestions for better building design:

- a simple layout
- ground floor only
- intersections of hallways marked by a nursing station
- circulation arranged in such a way that one always comes back in a loop to the elevator
- friendly staff to help the lost person

In their answers, however, none of the staff and volunteers mention signs, landmarks, or other ways of orienting which are particularly helpful to residents with impairments.

Part 3

Summary and suggestions

Many of the seniors described in Part 3 are socially isolated, and find it very difficult, if not impossible, not to feel "alone in a crowd." Whether you are a resident, family, friend, staff, or volunteer, there is something you can do now which might make a difference. The checklist in this section contains suggestions from the people who participated in the research project; there is space for adding *your* ideas.

Summary of Part 3 Findings

Part 3 shows that many of the seniors who live in care facilities have extra challenges compared with other residents or seniors in the community.

They may have physical impairments or economic circumstances which make it very difficult for them to cope with change, stay in touch with others, or even move around the care facility. These extra challenges affect whether these seniors can make and keep relationships. It is especially difficult, therefore, for them to become less socially isolated if they wish.

SUGGESTIONS FOR WHAT YOU CAN DO TO . . . make a difference to the senior who has extra challenges

Background Information:

Many of the seniors say that their impairments have a huge impact on their ability to do most things. The answers of family, friends, staff, and volunteers interviewed show that they may not be in touch with how the seniors feel physically and emotionally about impairments.

Ideas for Action:

Noticing Changes
- Look to see if there is a simple cause for a recent change — for example, a decrease in hearing may be a result of wax buildup in the ears
- Make sure that residents are regularly assessed for hearing and sight impairments and checked regularly for changes

- Lobby to extend the free audiology service now offered to Vancouver care facilities by the Vancouver/Richmond Health Board to all BC care facilities
- Help the person build on abilities and potentials (what he *can* do), rather than focusing only on limitations (what she *can't* do)
- When assessing the person who has impairments, communicate the results with the person as well as with staff, volunteers, family, and friends who are involved with him or her

- _____

- _____

Respect the Person
- Do not talk about the person as though he or she isn't present
- Use respectful language at all times
- Talk about the resident as a person first, not as a condition or impairment
- Always ask whether you can help; do not assume the person needs help
- Value the contributions of the residents
- Enjoy the residents as people

- _____

- _____

Help Compensate for Challenges
- Make name tags in large print for staff and volunteers, to help residents and family recognize them

- Be aware that some residents may no longer be able to read name tags or activities lists
- Be aware that many people with impairments do not like to ask for help
- Be aware that for a person with impairments, just getting around the building may be a constant challenge
- Sensitively explore ways that the resident who needs to ask others for help can "return the favour"
- Find out what kinds of visits work best for the person — maybe visit one at a time or for short periods of time
- Be sure that the residents have the proper necessities, such as an adequate supply of hearing aid batteries
- Work with the Family Council to create a fund which could be used to allow residents in reduced economic circumstances to go on outings or to make purchases

- _____
- _____

Training

- Make sure that staff, volunteers, family, and friends have as up-to-date training as possible about sensory losses — how to communicate with people who have hearing impairments; how visual impairments can lead to withdrawal; and what the loss of vision or hearing means to a senior on a deep and personal level

■ Remember that new residents and residents whose memories are slightly impaired may need some help to recognize others
■ Try to hire staff and recruit volunteers who speak more than one language

■ _____

■ _____

Avoid Stereotypes
■ Be aware that *everyone* has stereotypes about people who are old, blind, deaf, or have some visual or hearing impairment
■ Be aware that some people mistakenly believe that the elderly actually feel less pain or that they complain about pain unnecessarily
■ Be aware that residents who talk about pain or sadness are sometimes labelled "complainers"

■ _____

■ _____

Understanding the Effect of Impairments
■ Be aware that people with chronic pain will have "good" days and "bad" days, depending on how well the pain is under control
■ Be aware that the health and energy level of a person with impairments may change from day to day or hour to hour
■ Be aware that chronic pain and depression often go hand in hand
■ Be aware that residents may not talk about pain or sadness for fear of scaring off visitors

- Be aware that there are many alternatives to prescription drugs that can help with residents' pain — including hot packs, cold packs, relaxation imagery, music therapy, distraction, and biofeedback

- _____

- _____

Special Challenges of Dementia

- Learn more about the Gentlecare approach to people with dementia (see Moyra Jones, Helpful Reading in Appendix 2) and introduce it into the care facility
- Use non-verbal ways of communicating — for instance, hugs (always ask first); bringing children or a pet for a short visit; dancing or walking; hair brushing or nail care; bringing flowers, aromatic oils, perfumes, colourful cloth, books, tapes, fruit or other food treats

- _____

- _____

Part 4

Dignity of risk

This research project shows that doing something about social isolation of seniors in care facilities is not as simple as putting people together or adding activities and that being able to take risks is connected to social isolation. Just over one third of the seniors say that they want more control of their lives in some areas.

Some seniors feel that they have little or no control over their social isolation. This can mean the senior who wants to be more in touch with others and finds it very difficult. This can also mean the senior who prefers to be solitary, and finds it difficult having others respect this choice. Some of the seniors also find it difficult to control the impact of their impairments on their lives and especially on their relationships with others. Most seniors, however, control what they can. Part 1 shows that many residents take great pleasure in making decisions about their daily lives.

"I had to let my son take risks as he grew up; now it is time for him to let me do the same."

As the above quote shows, some seniors want to keep or take back their right to take certain risks. They have some support from others. In 1992, the National Advisory Council on Aging stated that every senior, whether living in the community or in a care facility, has the right to choose to live "at risk" as long as the senior is not found to be incompetent or likely to harm anyone else.

The term used for this right in care facilities is Dignity of Risk. For the senior who lives in a care facility, that might mean the following:
- to have chances to leave the care facility alone
- to travel on public transport, accompanied or unaccompanied
- to say that side-bars are not to be raised on the bed at night
- to stay in bed or in her room
- to get up when he wants
- to sit alone or with whom she wants in the dining room
- to drink alcohol in private
- to smoke
- to refuse food or medications

All of the above are examples of the freedoms which some seniors say they want and which some care facilities deny, regardless of the mental capacity of the senior. Management may fear legal consequences if the senior gets hurt. Families frequently request that the management of the care facility keep the seniors "safe," even if this means restricting their activities and refusing their requests. Staff are often faced with denying the seniors' requests and doing instead what management and families want. Even with the best of intentions, management, staff, volunteers, family, and friends may disagree among themselves about how much independence to "allow" the seniors.

As Part 1 has shown, staff, volunteers, family, and friends may gradually fall into a pattern of making decisions for residents or dissuading them from certain activities because they might harm themselves . . . or catch cold . . . or get overtired. The pattern may include plans for what the senior should or should not do if she or he is socially isolated. This is particularly true for seniors who say that they are lonely or who have one or more physical impairments. These seniors may not be able to do much about their impairments, and may already be finding it difficult to begin or keep relationships, and may find even their right to make decisions being taken away too. It is easy to see how this comes about.

As identified by the National Advisory Council, seniors who are not mentally competent or who may harm others do not have the right to live "at risk." Some people do not think the senior is competent if she or he wants to take any risks at all. On the other hand, making sure that the senior has control and respect for her or his choices may increase the chances that the senior will get hurt. And if taking the risk results in harm, is the senior the only person harmed?

What happens, for example, if the senior who has a mobility impairment refuses to have the side-rails raised on her or his bed and falls out and breaks a hip? Even if everyone agrees with the decision to leave the bed-rails down, it may be difficult to live with the consequences. The senior will be in pain and shock and have to go to the hospital. He may spend a long time in hospital and never regain his former level of physical health or mobility. She may lose her place in the care facility. The family must spend extra time visiting and supporting him in hospital, and perhaps finding a new care facility. Management may worry about being sued. If the senior does return to the care facility, staff has to spend extra time caring for her physically and helping her adjust to the care facility again.

Will the final result of this one senior taking a risk be that none of the residents in the care facility are ever again "allowed" to have their bed-rails down at night?

Or will the final result be that the other residents, management, family, friends, staff, and volunteers decide to continue together trying ways to make that senior's choice possible . . . whatever the consequences?

Epilogue

This epilogue comments on policies and programs which affect the operation of a care facility, but are outside the decision-making scope of the board or administrator of a care facility.

The goal of this research project has been to help understand life in care facilities and the needs expressed by seniors who live in them. The voices of the residents and others involved with them have directed our attention to the life inside the care facility. Throughout this handbook, we have offered suggestions based on these voices.

At the same time, we have learned that problems in care facilities — such as social

isolation and lack of chances to take risks —
need to be viewed in a broader context. The
Advisory Committee to this research project and
the Board of Directors of the Association of
Advocates for Care Reform (ACR) recognizes
that there are a number of important outside
influences on the lives of people who live in care
facilities.

Administrators may have the best of intentions,
but their hands are often tied by issues over
which they have little or no control — such as a
centralized waiting list for admissions, union
contracts, mortgage finances, and the linking of
funding to care levels. These issues make the
running of care facilities a daunting task. At the
same time, health boards and governments at all
levels must keep themselves accountable to the
general public not only for efficient and
economical use of public funds, but also for
standards in care.

In the final analysis, the care provided to
seniors in care facilities reflects the social
priorities of the society we all live in. The political
will needs to be there to bring about changes
which would make a difference to people who live
and work in care facilities — to continue to
monitor and improve care; to train staff; to offer
incentives for outstanding service; to reward
creative approaches, and to fund care facilities
adequately. At present, however, public attitudes
seem to make it politically undesirable to add

resources when setting priorities for health and social programs. Some who are involved with people who live in care facilities warn that such "false austerity" is short-sighted and may result in a self-perpetuating circle of increased social isolation, heavier care needs, family stresses, breakdowns from giving care beyond their personal energy and resources, longer hospitalizations, and on and on.

Over the course of this research project, there have been a number of changes in how care for seniors in care facilities is provided throughout British Columbia. For example, in the Lower Mainland, the Vancouver/Richmond Health Board now has a new role in overseeing the programs and budgets of care facilities. The Review of the Vancouver Continuing Care System and The Way Home Report (September 1996), the activities of the Seniors Population Health Advisory Committee, and media attention to the possible closing of two private care facilities all took place while we worked on this handbook. There continues to be discussion about amalgamation and budget reallocations throughout the province.

What does all this mean for the seniors whose voices speak to us in this research? Throughout this project, the seniors told us that they need to be more involved in the decisions that affect them. Some service providers tell us, however, that they must make all final decisions, and that seniors and the public have a limited role in suggesting changes. We admit that involving everyone in this kind of decision-making is not always easy or even pleasant, nor is it a cure for all ills. Nevertheless, this research project shows clearly that the personal experiences of seniors who live in care facilities provide a unique insight into both problems and solutions. Seniors should not be left out of the decision-making process.

Clearly, all is not ideal. Many suggestions throughout the handbook are directed to possible improvements within care facilities. Many people have offered great ideas and have shown how committed they are to improving care. Not all of their ideas require major changes in policy. Nevertheless, unless some changes can take place outside care facilities, many good and equitable ideas will come to nothing. While proper funding is crucial, putting more money into the system will not produce good results without also attending to fairness in staff training, employment standards, and communication across all decision-making levels. These types of changes do not happen quickly.

Who can speak for those residents and families who feel that they are not being heard? The Association of Advocates for Care Reform (ACR) encourages the development of Family Councils in care facilities, as ways of helping residents and their families have their concerns heard both in and outside of the care facility. Alternatives need to be considered as well, such as appointing for each care facility a senior ombudsperson or an arbitrator familiar with the issues of seniors who live in care facilities. This person or group would be independent of the various systems that affect the running of the care facility, and might be able to find solutions that others are not aware of, or overlook because they are too close to the problem.

Can the general public become more involved? We believe that there is a role for ACR and like-minded organizations to help raise everyone's awareness of the issues which affect seniors who live in care facilities. We welcome your ideas.

Appendix 1

The research project

The formal definition of social isolation used for the research project is: "the observed and perceived dimensions and outcomes of the presence or absence of residents' meaningful relationships with others."

How the Project Was Carried Out

Care Facilities: Four out of 11 randomly selected care facilities in the Lower Mainland participated in the research project. Each reviewed the interview questionnaire before giving final agreement to proceed. Three are intermediate care facilities and one is an extended care facility. They range in size from 75 to 120 residents.

One of the care facilities has four residents per room (with the possibility of private or semi-private at addltlonal charge). The others have private or semi-private rooms. The daily charge for each care facility depends on a preset sliding scale set by Continuing Care.

Most of the residents of the facilities are from the mainstream culture — Caucasian and English-speaking. In one of the care facilities, however, over 20 percent of the residents are Chinese.

Advisory Committee: The questionnaires were vetted by the 13 members of the Project Advisory committee, eight of whom are seniors. The Advisory Committee also reviewed the draft research report which was written by Darja Kiara and became the foundation for this handbook.

Volunteer Research Assistants (VRAs): The interviews were carried out by more than a dozen VRAs, approximately one half of whom were seniors. One VRA who conducted telephone interviews lives in a care facility himself. The VRAs were enlisted through several methods, including senior centres, personal contacts, and referrals. They were provided with one day of training. Other VRAs joined partway through the project and were trained individually. All of the residents were interviewed in person. Staff, family, friends, and volunteers were interviewed in person or by telephone.

Selection of Residents: The care facilities provided a list of potential participants considered cognitively and linguistically able to do the interviews. Care facility staff contacted each resident to explain the study, and if she or he agreed to participate, the VRA phoned the resident to schedule an interview at a mutually convenient time.

Interviews with the residents ranged from 45 minutes to over two hours. For some the interview was divided over two sessions to better accommodate the resident's energy or needs. Some interviews were more challenging than others, because of the resident's physical impairments, the length of the interview, or the lack of privacy, particularly in shared rooms.

Family, friends, staff, and volunteers were selected in a similar fashion. While all of the family and friends are people involved regularly with a senior who lives in a care facility, not all are involved with the seniors who participated in this research project. In this research project, the vast majority of family and friends interviewed are women. One half are daughters, and only one in five are husbands or sons.

A Profile of the Residents

The 49 residents interviewed range in age from 71 to 98. Forty-five percent are over 85 years old. Thirty-eight (77.5 percent) are women and 11 (22.5 percent) are men.

About one in four of the residents have always lived in British Columbia. The other residents come from the Canadian Prairies, the American Midwest, and Europe.

More than two thirds (68.8 percent) of the residents have had their spouses die; about one in five (14.6 percent) are single or never married; a few (8.7 percent) are still married or in long-time partnerships; and even fewer (6.3 percent) are divorced. Some have been married or in a long-time partnership for a long time — 54.3 percent have been married 40 or more years, although in some cases, this may have meant more than one marriage or partnership. The longest marriage was over 67 years.

Over one quarter of the residents (26.5 percent) have less than a grade six education and 49 percent have less than a grade nine education. On the other hand, 22.4 percent have post-high school training. The residents describe a wide range of work they have done throughout their lives — including homemaker, farmer, office worker, sales person, small business owner, foundry worker, pastor, store manager, dressmaker, beautician, cook, interior decorator, transport driver, domestic, accountant.

Limitations of the Research: This research project excluded seniors with dementia, (although family members of residents with dementia were included); non-English-speaking residents (and their families); and residents outside the Lower Mainland. As well, the research project excluded seniors who were not willing to participate and others who care facility staff considered unable to participate. This may have included seniors who are very lonely and isolated.

A Summary of the Project Findings

Project aims: The purpose of the project was four-fold: (1) to hear from seniors about their experiences living in care facilities; (2) to look at obvious and not-so-obvious causes of social isolation; (3) to gather suggestions about how to prevent or at least reduce social isolation of seniors in care facilities; and (4) to create this handbook about social isolation and distribute it widely to those interested in or affected by social isolation.

Major Findings:
- It is important to try to differentiate between people who are alone by preference and those who are alone for other reasons

- Doing something about social isolation of seniors in care facilities is not as simple as adding more people or activities

- Whether or not they are socially isolated, many of the seniors have at least a few important or meaningful relationships with others

- Many of the seniors say that they want more control over their lives and want their choices respected

- Many of the seniors say that impairments — physical, visual, hearing, low energy, and chronic pain — are major barriers to socializing, doing activities, and finding meaning in their lives

- Many of the seniors with extra challenges — for instance, seniors who have impairments — have already lost considerable control over parts of their lives

- Being able to take risks is connected to social isolation

- Doing something to support the senior who wants to take risks may be doing something about social isolation

Appendix 2

Information

HELPFUL READING

BOOKS:

Bianchi, Eugene. *Elder Wisdom: Crafting Your Own Elderhood*. New York: Crossroad, 1994.

Coughlan, Patricia. *Facing Alzheimers: Family Caregivers Speak*. New York: Ballantine Books, 1993.

Cusack, Sandra. *Isolated Seniors: Closer to Home Demonstration Project*. New Westminster Health Department, 1996. Phone: (604) 525-3661 or write: 537 Carnarvon Street, New Westminster BC V3L 1C2.

Doyle, Veronica. *It's My Turn Now.* Vancouver BC:
SFU Gerontology Centre, 1994.

Gubrium, Jaber. *Speaking of Life: Horizons of
Meaning for Nursing Home Residents.* New
York: Hawthorne, 1993.

Gruetzner, Howard. *Alzheimers: A Caregiver's
Guide and Sourcebook.* New York: John Wiley
and Sons, 1992.

Hay, Jennifer. *Alzheimers and Dementia:
Questions You Have—Answers You Need.*
Allentown, Pennsylvania: People's Medical
Society, 1996. (Other books in this series
include Arthritis, Stroke, Heart, and
Depression.)

Jones, Moyra. *Gentlecare: Changing the
Experience of Alzheimer's Disease in a
Positive Way.* Burnaby BC: Moyra Jones
Resources, 1996.

Kane, Rosalie and Alan Caplan, eds. *Everyday
Ethics: Resolving Dilemmas in Nursing Home
Life.* New York: Springer Publishers, 1990.

Nickerson, Betty. *Old and Smart: Women and the
Adventure of Aging.* Madeira Park BC: Harbour
Publishing, 1996.

Sarno, J. and M. Sarno. *Stroke: A Guide for Patients and Their Families.* New York: McGraw-Hill, 1979.

Spencer, Charmaine. *Risk and Seniors at Risk.* Ottawa ON: Prepared under contract for Canadian Association on Gerontology and Seniors Directorate, 1995.

Thompson, Wendy. *Aging is a Family Affair.* Toronto ON: N.C. Press, 1987.

Weiland, D., et al. *Cultural Diversity and Geriatric Care: Challenges to the Health Professions.* New York: Hawthorn, 1994.

BROCHURES, NEWSLETTERS, ARTICLES AND BOOKLETS:

Articles in *Expression*, National Advisory Council on Aging, Ottawa ON K1A 0K9:

- *Alternative Medicine and Seniors*, vol. 11, no. 2, Winter 1996-97;
- *Canada's Oldest Seniors: Maintaining the Quality of Their Lives*, 1992;
- *Living with Sensory Loss: Topical Texts on Vision, Smell and Taste, Hearing and Touch*, 1990;
- *Aging and the Meaning of Life*, 1992.

Assisting Elderly Victims of Abuse and Neglect.
BC Seniors Advisory Council, Office for
Seniors, 1992. Write: 1515 Blanshard, Victoria
BC V8W 3C8.

Caregiver News. Caregivers Association of BC.
Write: 170 - 216 Hastings, Penticton BC V2A
2V6.

Continuing Care Resources. Armour Health
Assoc., Box 124, Chemainus BC V0R 1K0.
(Published monthly. A valuable and up-to-date
resource.)

Developing Leisure Identities. (Ways to support
people with disabilities.) Judith McGill,
Brampton Caledon Community Living, 34
Church Street West, Brampton ON L6X 1H3.
Fax: 905-453-8853.

*Experience in Action: Community Programming
for Healthy Aging.* Centre for Health Promotion,
University of Toronto, 1997. Fact sheets on
Volunteers, Core Values, Community Change,
Participation and Leadership by Seniors.
Phone: (416) 978-1809; fax: (416) 971-1365.

Living with Vision Loss. Canadian National
Institute for the Blind, Lower Mainland- South
Coast- Fraser Valley. Several pamphlets with
specific suggestions for families, caregivers,
staff, and others. Phone: (604) 431-2121; fax:
431-2199.

Musings from a Dementia Unit. Irene Barnes, Dementia Care, 1995. Write: 401-3880 Quadra, Victoria BC V8X 1H4.

A New Home. G. Levi and B. Petty, 1992. Challenges of Later Life Series, YWCA, Vancouver. (Many other useful titles in this series.)

Reach for Health and Information for Seniors (2nd Ed). BC Ministry of Health and Ministry Responsible for Seniors, 1995. Phone: 1-800-665-4347 toll free.

Six Steps to Preventing Falls, 1996. University of Victoria, School of Nursing, Box 1700, Victoria BC V8W 2Y2. Manuals also available: Taking Steps, Stepping Out.

Social Isolation: Unit Based Activities for Impaired Elders. Winifred Windriver. In the *Journal of Gerontological Nursing,* March 1993, vol.19, no. 3, pages 15-21.

Stroke: A Guide for the Family and How Stroke Affects Behaviour. Heart and Stroke Foundation of BC and Yukon. Phone: (604) 736-4404 or 1-800-693-8008 toll free.

Thinking about a Care Facility and *Continuing Care and You.* Vancouver/Richmond Health Board, 1997. Translated into several languages. Other useful booklets are also available from

the local Health Units. In Vancouver/Richmond:
VRHB Library, 1060 West 8th,Vancouver BC
V6H 1C4. Phone: (604) 736-2036 or (604) 736-
2033.

Through Tara's Eyes. Alzheimer Society of BC,
Provincial Office, #20 - 601 West Cordova,
Vancouver BC V6B 1G1. Phone: (604) 681-
6530 or 1-800-667-3742 toll free; fax: 604-669-
6907. A story booklet for parents or teachers to
help young school children cope with
Alzheimer's Disease. (Other material available
at this address.)

HELPFUL PEOPLE

Whether you are a resident, family, friend, staff, or volunteer, these groups may help you find services. The numbers are verified as correct in the spring of 1997. Many of these groups have regional or provincial offices which you may access with the Vancouver phone number. See the previous section, Helpful Reading, for details about pamphlets.

EMERGENCIES:
Dial 911 (except in some areas of BC — check your phone book)

Association of Advocates for Care Reform (ACR)
#303 - 1212 West Broadway
Vancouver BC V6H 3V1
Phone: (604) 732-7734; fax: (604) 730-1015
e-mail: aacr@vcn.bc.ca
internet: www.vcn.bc.ca/acr

Alcohol and Drug Information and Referral Services
Phone: (604) 660-9382
Seniors Well-Aware Program (Outreach program for seniors with alcohol problems in the community or care facilities)
Phone: (604) 687-7927
411 Dunsmuir Street, 3rd Floor
Vancouver BC V6B 1X4

Arthritis Telephone Information
Phone: 1-800-667-2847 toll free
or (604) 879-7511

Alzheimer Society of BC
#20-601 West Cordova
Vancouver BC V6B 1G1
Phone: (604) 681-6530

BC Coalition of Persons with Disabilities
#204 - 456 West Broadway
Vancover BC V5Y 1R3
Phone: (604) 875-0188

BC Smile,
BC Seniors Medication Information Line
Free Service Mon-Fri 10am - 4pm
In Greater Vancouver, phone: (604) 822-1330; In
other areas, phone: 1-800-668-6233 toll free

BC Transit - General Information
Phone: (604) 521-0400
BC Transit handyDART (Lower Mainland)
This service is available in many other
communities as well.
HandyLine phone: (604) 433-5995
Bookings phone: (604) 430-2692

Cancer Information Line
Phone: (604) 879-2323

Canadian Hard of Hearing Association
1460 Matthews Street
Vancouver BC V6H 1W9
Phone: (604) 733-7314

Canadian Mental Health Association
#1200 - 1111 Melville Street
Vancouver BC V6E 3V6
Phone: (604) 688-3234

Canadian National Institute for the Blind
Lower Mainland-South Coast-Fraser Valley
100-5055 Joyce Street
Vancouver BC V5R 6B2
Phone: (604) 431-2121
BC-Yukon Division phone: (604) 431-2020
Phone for the Deaf TTY: (604) 431-2131
Other areas phone: 1-888-431-0111

Crisis Centre (24 hours)
Phone: (604) 872-3311

Denture Clinic, Academy of Dentistry
#1303-750 West Broadway
Vancouver BC V5Z 1J3
Phone: (604) 876-7311

Diabetes Information Line
1091 West 8th
Vancouver BC V6H 2V3
Phone: (604) 732-4636;
e-mail: cdabc@istar.cr;
internet: www.diabetes.ca

411 Seniors
Information and Counselling Service
411 Dunsmuir Street
Vancouver BC V6B 1X4
Phone: (604) 684-8171

Handicapped Parking Placard
#106a - 2182 West 12th
Vancouver BC V6K 2N4
Phone: (604) 736-4367; fax: (604) 736-8697

**Heart and Stroke Foundation
of BC & the Yukon**
1212 West Broadway
Vancouver BC V6H 3V2
Phone: (604) 736-4404;
internet: www.cais.net/naric/stroke.html

Information Services - The "Red Book"
(Information and referral service for non-profit
and community services throughout the Lower
Mainland)
#202 - 3102 Main Street
Vancouver BC V5T 3G7
Phone: (604) 875-6381;
e-mail: informbc@vcn.ca

**Intergenerational Program Resource
and Information Kit**
Vancouver School Board
Partners in Education
1678 West Broadway
Vancouver BC V6J 1X6
Phone: (604) 713-4500

Little Brothers - Friends of the Elderly
(International, non-denominational, non-profit, volunteer-based organization committed to relieving isolation and loneliness among the elderly)
internet: http://littlebrothers.org/internat/home.html#canada

Medic Alert Foundation
#301 - 250 Ferand Drive
Toronto ON M3C 3G8
Phone: 1-800-668-1507 toll free

MOSAIC (Multilingual Service)
1522 Commercial Drive
Vancouver BC V5L 3Y2
Phone: (604) 254-0244

Osteoporosis Resource Line
Phone: (604) 731-4997

Patient and Family Resource Centre
"Connections to Information"
Vancouver Hospital, Laurel Pavilion
855 West 12th
Vancouver BC V5Z 1M9
Phone: (604) 875-5887

Red Cross Equipment Loan
4750 Oak Street
Vancouver BC V6H 2N9
Phone: (604) 879-7551

Stroke Recovery Association of BC
Phone: (604) 688-5603

United Ostomy Association
Phone: (604) 430-1522 or (604) 738-7065

Vancouver/Richmond Health Board
(Also for information about videos which can be
viewed in-house or borrowed)
1060 West 8th
Vancouver BC V6H 1C4
Phone: (604) 736-2033

Vancouver Public Library
Outreach Services
(for talking books and home delivery)
2425 MacDonald Street
Vancouver BC V6K 3Y9
Phone: (604) 665-3984

Volunteers for Seniors
in Long Term Care
Vancouver/Richmond Health Board
1770 West 7th
Vancouver BC V6J 4Y6
Phone: (604) 734-1221

Volunteer Vancouver
Phone: (604) 875-9144

Western Institute for the Deaf
2125 West 7th
Vancouver BC V6K 1X9
Phone: (604) 736-7391

West Main Health Unit
Continuing Care/Volunteers
2110 West 43rd
Vancouver BC V6M 2E1
Phone: (604) 261-6366